We Need Each Other
Building Gift Community

Bill Kauth with **Zoe Alowan**

For David & Patt- We are so blessed by your radiant blessings. May this book of ours bless you in some way! Zoe & Bill

You never change something by fighting the existing reality. To change something, build a new model that makes the existing model obsolete.
Buckminster Fuller

Ninth Draft Edition: September 2011

Note: This book is a work in progress, not yet a completed project. However, it is fully adequate to share and begin putting value into the world. The authors would much appreciate any suggestions for additions or corrections.

Stay in touch: We invite you become a subscriber so we can include you in the conversation as we all develop better ways to build community. Please go to our website and click on subscribe.
http://www.weneedeachother.net/

ISBN 0974489093

Silver Light Publishing
1/18/10

ISBN # 978-0-9744890-9-4

Credits:
Cover design by Zoe Alowan with Nik Colyer.
Photos: Zoe Alowan and Bill Kauth
Chapter 4 artwork:
Appearance of the Firebird by Zoe Alowan

Work in Progress – Evolving Process

This book is the result of the authors many attempts to build community over several decades. It exists in this form as our highest truth about what has worked and might work to build community at this time in the history of our world.
As our **best practices network** continues to evolve this book will evolve. Please share your successes and failures as we learn and co-create together. You may contact us directly at this e-mail address: bkindman@mind.net

Dedication

This book is dedicated to our parents and children:
Ardell & Rita. Henry & Blanche
Joseph & Sarah, Asha & Ari

And to our many ManKind Project "brothers"
for your devotion, passion, and work
to bring healthy masculinity back into our world!

Acknowledgments

The people whom we bless as collaborators include Craig Comstock, Jeff Golden, Charles Eisenstein, Dianna Leafe Christian, Herb Rothschild, Margaret Shockley David Kaar, Alpha Lo, Wendy Fullerton, Jack Leishman, Nik & Barbara Colyer, Carol & Timothy Nobles, Tracy Sage, Steve Lawler and Chris Bullock.

For their influence on our understandings we are indebted to Jean Houston, David Korten, Richard Heinberg, Robert Augustus Masters, Richard Rohr, Neale Donald Walsh, David Gershon, Carolyn Schaffer, Robert Bly, Peter Block, Gordon Clay, Peter Senge, Marshall Rosenberg, Carolyn Myss, Carolyn Baker, John Michael Greer, Cecile Andrews, Robert Moore, Ken Wilber, Michael Dowd, Norma Burton and Kate & Rusty Lutz.

Table of Contents

How to Use This Book

It's a tool, friends, so write in it,
sharpen your interest, your passion calls you.
Take out your fishing line and cast into the River Gift.

It's a guidebook, friends, to follow the ins and outs
that inspire you to co-create community of heart;
to weave the nets and gather the sparks.

It's a movement, friends, that leads you to wonder
How is this lifeboat built?
What would be strong enough to hold the hearts
of Wildman and Wildwoman crewing together,
sailing the big waters, living the gift?"

Zoe Alowan

Introduction

*Never doubt that a thoughtful group of committed citizens
can change the world.
Indeed, it is the only thing that ever has.*

Margaret Mead

This book is designed to build trusting, long-term, face-to-face communities as safe social orders, which in turn generate the energy needed to build our new social systems. Though it sounds simple, it's complex and challenging. We have been working on the process of community building for decades, each in our own way and writing this book for years. Zoe graciously offers the feminine voice to balance the years of Bill's doing men's work. Her cover, art, chapters as well as editing are much in the flow of this book.

Note on "I & we": We use these interchangeably: working together we've become the "we" co-creating this body of work.

Note on writing style around gender: We will use **her** and **his** – **he** and **she** interchangeably. We honor the women's movement for bringing this profound awareness forward, only short decades ago.

We Need Each Other for Love and Support.

Love: We recognize that we have been so alienated from each other that our hearts are longing and calling out for connection. Here we find the intimacy, family, friends, and community we long for. **Here lives the love!**

Support: The disintegration of our social, economic, and environmental systems will require us to co-operate with each other in ways we can barely imagine. We will need each other more and more. In our core community, we know who we can really count on and who can really count on us. **Here lives the support!**

Book at a Glance

SECTION ONE: Overview and Context

OUR VISION: This book opens with a new model of "Core Gift Community" designed to be world changing. We meet the authors; Bill, his worldview, background, where is he coming from, and Zoe, who brings a feminine voice to this discussion.

WHAT IS COMMUNITY: We explore what community is in many forms and what's possible. The exploration then is placed in the context of the times we live in, the urgency of the task, and its transformational possibilities.

WHO ARE WE: This vision of community is being grounded by the people who are ready to live a "Gift" community. Just who are these people and what are their values, psychosocial and spiritual qualities? Here we find an invitation to step into the challenge of our times by creating something which reflects an increasingly visible new worldview. We consider what values might be shared and how we might love, protect and indeed need each other.

OUR STORY OF LOST COMMUNITY: We take a fierce look at reasons why community seems to have vanished and why people are so rarely living their gifts We explore the economic, psychological and political forces in our culture that actually sabotage community.

SECTION TWO: How to Build Your Community

WHO VISIONS: We explore the actual process, which starts with a champion who holds the vision, sets the values, and offers the basic structure.

COMMITMENTS: We advocate a bonded type of community that has in-depth commitments to each other, place, time, gender safety, and shared core values.

MEMBERSHIP: We work through the complexities of membership, such as finding, welcoming, evaluating readiness, selecting, and establishing the "gates" on their path to initiation.

SECTION ONE: CONTEXT

Charles leads us to a grand vision of Gift Culture

PART 1

VISION AND OVERVIEW

Chapter 1 Proposal and Premises

In a shift similar to that which nature makes–
humanity is being challenged to make a jump
to a new level of community.

Duane Elgin

Proposal

Establish "core communities" designed to co-create "gift culture."

The **"core"** is the special group of people chosen as family to be with, share with, laugh and cry with. The **"gift"** is the focus on "what can I give." The word **"community"** comes from the Latin word *cum-munere—munere* meaning "to give" and *cum* meaning "among each other." So, **"to give among each other"** is a useful way to think about community.

Vision of Our Core Gift Community: We're a local, non-residential, committed, intimate, bonded, tribe of men and women supporting each other as we build the new gift culture.

<u>Defining components of the vision</u>

Gift Culture: This appears to be the emerging worldview as humanity matures. We can see the transition of values moving from transaction to trust, from consumption to contribution, from scarcity to abundance and most relevant to this book - from isolation to community.

Gift community: Rooted in the values of the Gift Culture, it both recognizes that we need each other and honors our need for autonomy. It's a "fictive kinship" in which people choose each other in a kind of tribal family. We support each giving their gift, especially new social inventions.

Core Community: Describes the tribe of choice with whom we spend our time and invest our hearts.

Local: Connected and committed to staying in one place. We live within a few square miles (roughly bicycling distance) of each other.

Non-residential: We mostly do not live on the same property, but can visit each other easily and often.

Committed: We choose each other and make clear agreements to stay together for a "long time"—ideally a lifetime

Intimate: We feel safe, and love and trust each other as in a healthy marriage. Our authenticity and integrity shine.

Bonded: Our basic focus, after family, is with each other. We consider the well-being of our tribe/core first.

Tribe/core: Between 30-150 people, we hold each other as family, yet we're bigger than family, bonded in an archetypal, visceral level beyond words.

Men and women: The time has come for both genders to feel safe and respected with each other, like close sisters and brothers.

Action in the world: We support each other as conscious, creative people actively building a new gift culture based on these new values.

Premises

Our current culture and its systems are rooted in premises (beliefs or memes) that no longer serve us. We believe that the following premises to be necessary in establishing stable community:

- Humans most want love, family, friends and community.
- We come to love and trust those with whom we are most transparent and spend the most time.
- Commitments help build enduring relationships and community.
- Staying in place is essential to the possibility of authentic community.
- We can effectively choose the tribe we feel best with.
- A relationship with energies of the Great Mystery informs our work.
- It is now possible for women and men to be safe with each other, practicing transparency and observing clear boundaries.
- We prefer fewer deep, close friends rather to many casual acquaintances.
- Knowing and bonding with each other in part depends on the amount of quality time spent together.
- Current social and economic uncertainty suggests we will be well served by forming mutual safety nets.
- Once authentically happy, each of us will move towards creating the new world.
- We see the need, and feel called to serve, in the co-creation of a new culture that honors all life.

We are aware that our proposed **"Core-Gift Community"** model is different from anything that has been popular in the last few decades. Because it is highly intentional and includes structure, commitment, and membership, it may make some people bristle with anxiety or perhaps feel some fear of being overpowered or betrayed. Others may object on principle to anything that is not completely inclusive.

We invite you to hold the tension of opposites and stay open to a new possibility.

We use some of the best learning from years of co-housing and eco-villages adapted to non-residential situations. On the shoulders of those pioneers we co-create our future. We trust that within the safety of our core community the needed social, economic, environmental and other "safety-net" inventions will become practical and support the balance of all life.

Chapter 2   Reclaiming Each Other

"The creation of a core community is a powerful answer
to our collective crisis of isolation and alienation.

Because we live in the belly of a soul-eating culture,
we face enormous pressures every day to adjust,
accommodate and abandon our essential self.

Coming into the shelter of our own village
or core community is one way
to protect our intrinsic value
and restore our indigenous soul."

Francis Weller

If you can feel the deep truth of the above quote, I invite you to consider living into the possibility of a **core gift community.**

Most research indicates that, when we ask people what they really want, they always say love, family and a community of friends. It's what we all want. Given this deep hunger for community, why is it NOT available and how might we open ourselves to the community we have been longing for?

Why is it so hard? The answer is that our current culture conveys the message that **WE DO NOT NEED EACH OTHER.** The truth is that **WE DO NEED EACH OTHER**, now more than in over a century. Subsequent chapters in Section One, especially Part 4 explores how our consumer culture has hijacked our ability to bond with each other and how, as we learn to live more fully in community, we might come to know that we do indeed need each other.

Social, psychological, political, and economic design factors are all in play here. As I speak with fellow elders, we recall a once vital sense of community that has been lost. And it is lost forever. We can't simply go back to what we remember. Our circumstances have evolved well beyond that. We must create something as yet unknown. Some of us see the current dramatic world changes as offering possibilities for utterly new and more mature kinds of community. We have dared to hope for the designs that are just now beginning to evolve.

The times in which we live feel so scary, yet they are so ripe, so ready to birth deep community as never seen before. Just as data technology has advanced over fifty years from a room-sized card calculator to a hand-held chip computer a thousand times more powerful, so have human relationship skills evolved dramatically.

Given the world situation, we must take seriously the challenge of using our refined relationship skills to build long-term, loving community! We do this so that we can feel safer, experience more joy, build a future, build a new culture.

But something is in the way. Why does it seem as if we do not need each other? What are our inner blocks to authentic community? Are we far more entranced by the current system than we realize? Can we imagine a possibility that does not yet exist? If we dare to see a new vision, we can move toward what we truly want.

As we discover our own courage to need each other, really need each other, and the awesome power to truly be with each other, men and women face to face, then we will discover how we can give our gifts and meet each others' needs. So many of our unmet needs for beauty, intimacy, love, support, safety, and play are waiting to be fulfilled.

As we accept this challenge, we might just change the world. Most people are willing to unplug from the system only when they see repeated examples of a better way to live. They need to see a workable alternative and feel invited to walk towards something better, not away from something bad. Those of us who are already, as Gandhi said, "becoming the change we want to see," might just be the inspiration for those who follow.

From the Tamera community in Portugal:
> Functioning community is the foundation of every humane transformation: human community and the community amongst humans and their fellow creatures. A universal way of being, which re-connects us with the sources of creation, can only be sustainably developed upon the foundations of an existence that is principally communitarian, not private. The paradigm shift, which is necessary for this is thus one of our core tasks.

Chapter 3   Why Me, Why Now?

At this time of supreme testing, we are being challenged to give nothing less than our highest and best gifts to the world.

Duane Elgin

When I read a book I always want to know, "Who is this author, what is her background, where did she get their ideas and who are her friends?" Having that context allows me to sort out the relative level of truth or wisdom I can expect. In that spirit I want to offer some sense of who I am in the world and in my heart. And because I'm making assertions and "professing" ideas that I believe are true, I want you to know how I've come to be influenced in finding my own truth. This will help you know who this book was designed for.

> "Friends, community, and personal growth all sound wonderful, but is it going to change the world?' you ask. Some medical people have been saying that there are people in our society who are literally dying of loneliness. And why not—what is there to live for if not for other people and love? TV? A new car? Am I saying, change or die"? Well, in a way, yes I am. People living in an alienated world without connection to other people tend to act in ways destructive to themselves and our planet. In their desperation to feel OK, too often they will abuse themselves or others. Scared people caught up in the shame could kill us all. Those who continue to build nuclear bombs, cut down rain forests and dump toxic wastes are examples. Those of us who stay ignorant or do nothing are passively supporting the way it is. Perhaps we humans do need to change to continue to live on our planet."

The quote above is from *A Circle of Men*, a book I published with St. Martins Press in 1992, nearly twenty years ago. Rereading it in 2010, especially the last sentence touched me to tears. We have not yet changed enough to protect our life-supporting planet. So what can we do?

I know the answer only for me. Building personal community, writing this book, now, at this time in my life is my calling. Given who I am, the very best use of my life energy is this book. It is the best gift I have to give. Indeed for me, it is the most important work in the world, right now.

Allow me to share a brief history. For thirty years I've been a social pioneer hacking through the underbrush of human bonding, arriving at amazing successes as well as many disappointing dead ends. This accumulation of lived experiences has informed me about what does and what does <u>not</u> work.

In the mid 1970s, as part of a men's support group I found a kind of safe closeness with men I had not known before. I was also a feminist therapist, which meant relating through authentic relationship. And I was becoming alerted to the world political situation. These three experiences led, in spring of 1984, to a "call" to do something for men. I invited two friends with great hearts.

Ron Hering, Rich Tosi and I, fairly simple guys from the Midwest, yet each with our own genius, somehow allowed the **New Warrior Training Adventure (NWTA)** to flow through us into the world. Seeing the potency of the training, we realized that the men needed on-going support and bonding, so we developed the **Integration Groups (I-groups).** These weekly groups were designed for men to sustain their inner learning process, so they tended to stay together for years. Many have lasted ten to twenty years.

Very organically, training centers emerged, and by the early 1990s we had a coast-to-coast presence, just about the time Robert Bly's book *Iron John* sold a million copies. Men were hungry for something, and the number of our centers tripled quickly. It was obvious that we offered something men really wanted. To feel their own deep sense of manhood, masculinity blessed by other men, is archetypically enlivening. Finding our hearts, trusting other men and feeling our life missions come alive also brought men to a new way of being.

By 2000 we had taken on the name **ManKind Project (MKP)** and were getting established around the world. As of 2010 we have served nearly 50,000 men via flourishing centers in eight countries. Our essence is service and integrity. Around the globe we have hundreds of splendidly trained leaders and an administrative system that works primarily by loving consensus. I feel very proud and hold these brothers as amazing. There is a more detailed history of MKP in Chapter 51.

For fifteen years I have served for MKP as Visionary-at-Large. In this role I studied intensely on a daily basis the "state of the world." At every annual meeting I report to my brothers what I have observed. As I dug deeper down the rabbit hole, each year I would return saying, "Brothers, remember how bad I said it was back last year, well it's worse." I could see economic, energy, and environmental collapses as inevitable and wanted to alert my brothers. In 2005 I visited 25 cities, meeting in groups of 15 to 50 men and women. Everywhere I could feel both the general fear and the anxious longing for community.

Between wanting to serve my brothers with my best gifts, feeling a bit too much like Chicken Little, and having some powerful experiences of intimate community, I felt called to bring forward communities of men and women. I yearned in particular for a deeper local community of close long-term friends, and I knew from many conversations the same yearning in so many others.

With MKP we already have an established brotherhood of tens of thousands of conscious men. Many are bonded in their I-groups, but I wondered, might it be possible for both men and women to bond? The wondering turned to action. Lots of research yielded the daunting discovery that there is not much out there and "if it is gonna get done, I'll have to do it." You too may have known this feeling.

Just build community! How hard can that be? Well, the list of failed attempts lengthy. But each noble experiment bettered our understanding of what might work next time. This book is full of much of this hard-earned wisdom.

JUST ANOTHER DAY IN PARADOX

I hold both an awareness of the fragility of our world for ourselves, our children, and grandchildren, and of its divine possibility beyond my capacity to comprehend. I know I share this paradox with billions of others as the immune system of Gaia leaps into action. Gift communities are one potent manifestation of the essential goodness of humankind to protect and care for others. I believe we are highly empathetic beings looking for the ways and structures through which we can use our extraordinary hearts and skills.

Most of the writers and theoreticians whom I respect say some variation of, "if we make it . . . " They have found the courage to recognize the environmental, energy, and economic dangers facing us and future generations. The outlook is stark and hard to swallow. Yet, because of the internet, many millions of us do know the painful facts. And there are tens of thousands of suggestions about what to do, ranging from business as usual to finding another planet. Eventually though, the challenge gets personal.

What will I do? Somewhere among all the desperate, brilliant, silly, and simple down-home proposals I sit with my own answer. It goes something like this:

9

Community as tribal kinship is the best way I can imagine to accelerate the rate of reconnection and the consequent changes needed to protect the planet and our grandchildren. I believe that via deliberate community we can reconnect and support each other in giving our gifts to make a sufficiently big difference.

And the really good news is that we are hard wired to do this. The answer to the hunger so many of us feel is in our genes. We cannot delude ourselves any more that we can go it alone. We know we must build the new society, and doing so starts with community. And community means tribe. The family is actually not the fundamental unit of society. It is the tribe. Tribe is who we are. We must recreate it. This is our time and this time is calling us.

My reality. Finally, to know me, you should know how I know what is real. We each have our own way of choosing what we believe is real, so I want to share the glasses through which I see life. As I tell you my basic philosophy of life, my metaphysical take on our world, you can know how I find my truth. Because I'm professing a view of reality and suggesting certain behaviors, you should know the source.

Over the years I've learned to observe the "sea of memes" in which our collective reality rests. We can call these worldviews or the larger beliefs with which we make sense of our decisions. I've come to trust both my intuition and my rational cognitive process to work together.

When new ideas show up, I want to know both rationally and intuitively just who is this person professing this belief, this idea? The internet allows me to Google and get information. Often if the book or new idea feels important enough I reach out and make personal contact with the author. Most of the books and websites in the lists of recommendations (see AFTERWORD) are the work of people with whom I've spent enough time to have touched-hearts in a way sufficient for me to trust them.

For example, I had come to know Richard Heinberg both personally and from many years of reading his monthly Museletter. So when his research uncovered "Peak Oil" and he took his learning public I trusted both his heart and his academic rigor. Having this insight about him opened doors to other authors whom he knows and trusts with a similar message and the courage to put it out publically.

On the cognitive level I have studied certain social, political areas with the many hundreds of hours needed to make a discriminating decision as to what feels deeply

99% true. From that vantage point I can view other authors or researchers as to their depth of insight or gaps in their knowledge base. This allows me some reasonable judgment as to how much to trust what they profess.

In all of my "truth" I also hold the possibility that I am wrong. I hold everything as my highest truth as of today. If someone shows me an idea or reality that is simply superior to the one I've been holding, I adopt it. And I believe we should test ourselves. If we stay too insular, we may not trust our truth. Over the last two years I had a rare opportunity to be in a very safe group with a brilliant man who holds Ayn Rand as his highest ideal. Because I hold her philosophy as the epitome of the obsolete story that has brought us to the edge of destruction it was with trepidation that I entered into hours of intense discussion. That interaction was so very useful for me, because I discovered that even under extreme challenge, my truth held strong. And, I suspect, so did his for him. It was not about win/lose, but rather about affirming the best truth each of us could know.

In your experience of this book I ask you to hold me to these same standards. Relationship is what it's all about. Do you know me, can you feel my heart? Do you know and trust the people I know and trust? Does what I hold as true resonate with some essential "truths" that you hold? Are you willing to stretch into a new possibility? Can you feel your fears and doubts and still hold a vision? In your heart you'll know if we can play together. If you do, read on and enjoy!

With all that said, I want to end this section with my basic beliefs summed up in one paragraph.

I believe that we humans are good, kind, compassionate, and empathetic beings. Our essential human nature has been disconnected from Earth. The resulting separate identity has led to *both* self-centered abuse and self-transcendent individuation. The abuse has now brought the planet of sentient beings into mortal danger, and at the same time given humankind an opportunity to take a leap of maturity into consciously serving all life.

11

Chapter 4   Zoe - the Feminine Voice: Our History

"Let your river run sister. It is not what you think. There is still life waiting for the miracle of grace and the touch of springtime long buried but never vanquished."

ALisa Starkweather

Reading an early version of Bill's manuscript for We Need Each Other, I stopped to gaze into the evening fire and it occurred to me that a woman's voice, my voice, was called for in this book about circles of men and women together. How obvious, you might say. Yes, obvious, but not easy, as I felt the need to speak to some of the difficulties of being immersed in the work of drawing people together. Our life revolves around this work and Bill's unrelenting focus on it as a vitally important social invention. Being a serious artist while in the midst of "Gift Community Central" is challenging and I struggle to claim time for teaching and painting. Also, as a menopausal woman who has spent her life giving and caring for others I can't ignore the voice that says "No. I do not want to see anybody right now. I need to be alone with the earth, quiet, singing or painting, but not with people, not today." This need for inner voice listening accompanies my enthusiasm and dedication for building gift community. I actively support women and men to stretch into the demands that community brings and to also know their limits and ask for what they need. This way there is actually room for building a sane and respectful community that balances the riches of collective group engagement with the riches that come from individual autonomy, self-knowing and deepening.

Her Story: A new community journey begins: Stepping into a weeklong experience of men and women together called Clearing the Air, I was filled with trepidation. The prerequisite trainings of both Healing the Father Wound and Healing the Mother Wound had been with other women. Sweet open-hearted connection had developed as we recognized our shared patterns of limitation and supported each other releasing old stories and hurts. But, was it possible to open up in the presence of men? During an early break, one of the women spoke saying, "We are so lucky. Most of the men are Warrior Brothers!" This meant nothing to me at the time. But over the course of the week I experienced how much more emotionally available and capable of transparency these Warrior Brothers of MKP were compared to those who hadn't had that experience with its skill sets.

Clearing the Air, focused on clearing up the swampland of misunderstanding and hurt between men and women. Before the beginning of the training, the signing of an agreement was required. Each of the sixteen people agreed to never be sexual with anyone in their group. This challenging agreement sparked a tremendous amount of discussion. Especially potent, the word "never" brought up: *"Nobody is going to tell me what I can or cannot do, forever. What if I meet my life partner there? How do you define 'never'? Does that mean three months, six months, one year? What happens if I can't resist the attraction? Does that mean I will need to become secretive, banished from the group? Or move into even greater transparency somehow?"*

It was a curious thing, but with that shared agreement, a remarkable opportunity for safety was established. Because much of our sexual posturing and courting behavior was locked into place as teenagers, this shared agreement offered a rare zone of opportunity. Fairly quickly, our old sexual strategy patterns dropped away sufficiently so that we could begin to be genuinely open, angry, fiercely truth telling, inquisitive, empathetic and self-owning. The safety of the space held and honed over the years by founder Gordon Clay and Shauna Wilson combined with the breadth of the inner work we did as a group showed me the possibility that men and women can reconnect with each other as truthful and courageous, honoring of our gender differences, yet available and intimate FRIENDS. My capacity to trust men, women and myself has only grown since this time.

For thousands of years what a terrible cycle has been playing out. It was only ninety years ago that women in America were imprisoned and tortured for declaring their right to vote. The patriarchy has and continues to encourage men to rape, scar and kill women as a form of power over in every war of land domination. This odd behavior, based perhaps on the twisted premise that men are superior to women, has also damaged the feminine spirit, the inner feminine aspect of men and the very body of the Mother Earth to horrific detriment. In turn, women have internalized this predation and have harbored a deep-seated anger and disdain for men. This turns all too often into manipulative emasculation by covert and overt shaming. In Clearing the Air, I was shocked to learn of rampant sexual abuse of boys by men and women. All this creates suffering, despair and further hatred. If we are to end war on this planet we must first heal the war that exists between the genders. In order to reclaim each other we need to honor and celebrate our differences. We need to take a stand to live beyond gender prejudice, self-owning the times when we do slip up. As we do this it is possible to reclaim each other and rebuild trust.

Notes on "trusting" from my dream journal: I am walking blindfolded, hand in hand in a procession of men and women. We are all blindfolded except for our guides, a man and a woman. I feel disoriented and clumsy as I attempt to find my gait. We begin to walk beside flowing water. I can hear it trilling and rippling at my side. Suddenly, I see all of us with eagle vision from above. We are a snaking chain of man, woman, man, woman, all who have released venomous anger and shameful secrets. We are open, loving and vulnerable. Suddenly, I am terrified. Without my sight, yet moving forward into the unknown, I am reminded of being led to the gas chambers. How can I trust when this terror is rising up. Horrible scenes of another time shake me to the core; a time when I stopped trusting anything... I let this feeling move in me while I hold more securely the hand of the man ahead of me. We arrive somewhere, a building perhaps. As we enter, still blindfolded, I step through wafts of sweet smelling sage. There is silence. Then, seemingly out of nowhere, whispering voices of men and women speak into my ear, "Welcome home. ...Welcome to your community.... We have been waiting for you." I burst into tears and wake up.

So Why Me, Why Now? Why am I so engaged in this core community building of men and women? In August 2005, friends gifted me with an experience of Burning Man. There you step into a world where everything but coffee and ice, and your own basic essentials of food and shelter is gifted-- art, showers, massages, teaching, performance, etc. It was there that I was introduced to this guy, Bill Kauth, and we spent a long night talking and preparing graham cracker, melted chocolate and marshmallow s'mores for hundreds of travelers on the dusty road past the camp. When he got up to leave I tenderly wiped melted marshmallow from his beard as though we had been married for twenty years.

Then, some three months later my dearest women friends gifted me with a trip to the ancient Goddess temples of Malta. In these six thousand year old circles of standing stones we joined twenty modern day priestesses in ritual around the divine feminine. On November first, after a breath-work session I experienced a deep inner cleansing and the words "You have work to do with Bill Kauth." I found this quite surprising. Upon returning to the states, I found his number and gave him a call, and indeed he had been holding me in his heart. After six months of extraordinary friendship we realized our work involved a deeply personal relationship. We declared this and celebrated with a group of friends.

Answering the Call: There is a Russian tale that storyteller, Michael Meade tells, called, "The Firebird", which begins with an ordinary fellow out on a ride with his extraordinary horse. They are on the path riding through the mountains when suddenly the man notices an unusual, eerie silence and sees before him, right in his way, the feather of a Firebird. This pulls them to a stop and he bends forward to look at it. His horse speaks saying, "I wouldn't pick up that feather if I were you, because if you do you will know pain and suffering." But what do you think? Does he pick it up? Of course he does. He is drawn to answer the opportunity, the call. Michael Mead often queries his audience, asking , "So, when did you pick up the feather? What feather was it? Drugs, meditation, a big project, bungee jumping? What was the cost?"

When I drove from California to Oregon to join Bill, I picked up the feather. On this memorable occasion the inspiring music of "Soul Fire" by New Zealand artist, Peru, was enveloping me. As my car rounded the bend, a stunning vision of Mt. Shasta, spectacular in early spring all capped with snow and set against a blue sky

exploded into view. Simultaneously, a vision of a new society seemed suddenly quite possible. A culture rooted in gratitude and loving respect for each other, for the sacred earth where people lived beyond prejudice, in balanced harmony. With this vision I also glimpsed the role that I could play in making this a reality. It felt overwhelming, very challenging, but so beautiful that all thought of any suffering or pain that might accompany this mission melted away. Really, I think there should be a notice on this section of Interstate 5: "Warning! Shockingly beautiful vista next bend! Prepare to take appropriate measures."

But what appropriate measures can you really take? In the Firebird story, even as you weigh the costs of suffering with the chances of success there is this unreasonable knowing that it's yours to do. The cautioning voice of the wise companion horse helps the hero champion part of us out, even when things become dire. It's been my experience that the universe is quite alive and responsive to our deepest prayers and longings. It does, however, seem to require greater and greater levels of trust and letting go.

In that Mount Shasta moment I let go of my past and opened to something unknown. Perhaps it was the multiple impact of music, inspired lyrics, a vision of beauty and a heart filled with new love. I am sure people the world over have had similar moments, experienced similar visions of something so awe inspiring and sweepingly grandiose that one feels it should be kept to oneself. Who would believe you? Even as I muttered to myself, that this was too outlandish, I answered the call. I picked up the feather of building new community as I headed over the mountain into Ashland and a new life with Bill.

Our History

> *"Life has taught us that love does not consist in gazing at each other, but in looking outward together in the same direction."*
> Antoine de Saint-Exupery

Champions Choosing Each Other

Diving into the Creative Pool: In the early days of our community building adventure, Bill and I were fortunate to join together with Norma Burton to develop a way of birthing this new vision. She brought tremendous courage, passion, devotion and vision to our team and a deeply grounded feminist perspective. We all had a great deal to learn from each other and our work was rich and full of promise. For over a year we met weekly; brainstorming, sharing, celebrating and diving into examining our shadows. Bill was plunged into an intense learning curve as he navigated the waters of collaborative partnership with two women. We attempted to impart to him the feminine perspective, elucidating how different it was from that of a patriarchal, privileged, white male. We formed a bonded collaborative friendship.

However, it can happen that champions who choose each other can proceed with the best of intentions yet actually want different things. Bill devoted himself to research and writing and was often frustrated that he couldn't find an existing model or a tangible structure for the community template. He concluded that what was essential to build trust and safety in the communities that we were envisioning was the need for bonding in small, selective groups. After presenting several weekend seminars where we explored people's longing for community, the idea of commitment to place and selectivity became even more significant. We built interest but the aspect of careful vetting began to trigger concern and misunderstanding between our core of three. Although we were in astonishing alignment in so many places, we were not in agreement around the issue of selectivity versus inclusivity. This was a very key element. Each approach has its virtues and pitfalls. Many important great works in the world can only thrive with the embracing arms of inclusivity, where all are welcome. Equally, tremendous brilliance that eventually comes to serve people throughout the world can often only begin its growth in conditions of contained safety and support.

After many efforts to reconcile the differences our little threesome disbanded. It is painful when champions discover that they want different things but through this time and process, the seeds of our community had been sown.

Community Building Symposium: In 2008, after the set back with our disbanded team, Bill and I went on to host a Community Building Symposium. Since we were questioning our own expertise, we called in a bona fide expert, Diana Leafe Christian. Wikipedia describes her as "an author, former editor of *Communities* magazine, and a national speaker and workshop presenter on starting new ecovillages and community and sustainability. She lives in an off-grid homestead at Earthhaven Ecovillage in the Blue Ridge Mountains of North Carolina. We were joined in planning and facilitating this three-day residential experience by Carolyn Shaffer, author of *Creating Community Anywhere,* and MKP leader, David Kaar. Together with Diana, we opened up the whole question of building community in a very productive way.

Diana brought us face to face with two of the biggest challenges that face community building. The first is, "Shared Vision/Shared Outcome" and second, the need for "Potential Member Evaluation." In regard to vision and outcome, she engaged the fifty people in some creative theater role-playing. One person was assigned the role of alternative energy fanatic, the second, a person focused on emotional processing, and the third, a person who was drawn to community for its spiritual connections. The outcome was quite humorous, but demonstrated how important it is to clearly determine if your shared outcomes are the same. Otherwise, sooner or later, the newly formed community goes nowhere due to the stress of really not wanting the same thing.

As to member evaluation, Diana presented disquieting information. She shared situation after situation where one person completely brought down an otherwise successful community. She emphasized the importance of background checks, contacting personal references and giving a time period for getting acquainted. This was quite challenging to many of the participants and she agreed that it is a hard thing for the generation of the sixties to be hard nosed and practical about qualifying people. She also advised that the ideal core group to begin with is between three to five people. Too many people feels like too many cooks spoiling the soup.

Diana's substantial knowledge included a wide range of practical suggestions and expertise from choosing members to agreements around individual and group rights. We added exercises and processes about how community has touched each of our lives. We also considered such difficult subjects as "Who might the people be who you would feed and house for a month, three months, a year, etc.?" The symposium was quite dynamic and we were extremely grateful for the opportunity the Symposium offered.

We handled the money in a way that was new to me. Bill suggested collecting hard costs up front with the registration then advising people that at the end of the symposium we would distribute feedback forms and ask them to gift the facilitators based on their ability to pay and on the value that they felt they had received. This was a three-day event and all food was included. The chefs for the occasion consisted of two fine cooks: David Kaar's partner Joanne, and myself. This cooking part was intended to provide for the varied diet restrictions of the attendees while offering them the healthiest and most delicious food at the lowest cost. We donated our time and cooked for two days. The food was wonderful. I wanted to create the ambiance of a family with everyone eating together. The lesson learned was also wonderful. I realized that my days of cooking for over fifty, organizing, facilitating, serving and cleaning up are over. It was ridiculously self sacrificing and unsustainable. The contributions that people made varied widely according to ability to pay, but it all evened out and we were able to pay our presenter well. Most people just filled our hearts to brimming with their comments and generosity. However, there were two whom I would not recommend for another such event. They were inappropriate, deceitful and energetically expensive. Because we had not been sufficiently selective we got to experience the sort of dysfunction Diana had warned us about.

Seeding the Gift Culture: Following the Symposium, Bill turned his attention to writing and researching on the Internet even more extensively. One day he made a louder than usual expression of delight from his computer cave. He had discovered the work of Charles Eisenstein and promptly ordered his book, "The Ascent of Humanity." Of course he liked it so much, that he contacted Charles, a young man in his early forties, and soon a case of Chuck's insightful books arrived at our door. There was something so profound about the way Charles talked about the Gift Culture that Bill invited him to fly from Pennsylvania to offer a workshop in Ashland on Gift Economy. Charles attracted young thinkers in their twenties as well as well as middle aged people and elders. It was very engaging to sit in circle with this diverse population and share common ground.

Charles' workshop on Sacred Economics was so well received, that soon Bill engaged two other visionary brothers, Rod Newton and Will Wilkinson to join him in planning a five-day September retreat with Charles. They began to meet weekly and Bill worked on it every day. Informed by our learning experience with Diana at our Community Symposium, Bill undertook the task of carefully interviewing the registrants to be sure we were aligned in our interest. When what we called, *Seeding the Gift Culture* was ready to commence, we realized that we had exactly fifteen men and fifteen women. Buckhorn Springs, an old restored retreat center outside of town was the perfect place to host us. Seven of us were on staff. The three planners and their uniquely competent wives (Brooks, Tashina and myself) joined Charles in offering a rich, mind opening, heart expanding journey into a new way of holding the Earth, each other and our culture.

We turned a corner from focusing on collapsing environmental, economic and energy systems to stand in the abundance of our natural gifts and our ability to give back to each other and our Lover Earth. We danced, sang and released old stories of separation and greed as we listened to Charles point out a new paradigm shift into Gifting and accepting ourselves as The Gift. As we were learning from Charles, I watched how Charles was, in turn being mentored, especially by Bill and Rod. We all added to each other's deepening in such a beautiful way that by the end of our four days we accomplished a small miracle. Just before dawn we all ascended a steep mountain. (See photo-Section One page 1). We moved so slowly and collectively that everyone, even those with some physical restrictions and the elderly, were able to climb to the summit of the mountain to a flat meadow. There, Bill and Charles initiated us as seeders of the Gift Culture. It was gloriously beautiful from that majestic vantage point. Then we carefully descended, caring for the well being of the whole group each step of the way.

People are capable of so much depth. Humanity is an untapped resource just waiting for a mythic purpose and integrity to call them to their greatest joy. From this Seeding the Gift Culture retreat the most excellent creations are flowering. One man has started The Gifting Tree Wellness Center, a Gift Clinic. In Ashland we are holding monthly Gift Circles that are sparking all sorts of networking, camaraderie and change. Another man from the retreat, Alpha Lo, has composed a booklet on Gift Circles and has inspired circles at Yale University in New Haven, Connecticut and in Chicago, Illinois. Charles has lead three more Seeding the Gift Culture retreats and Bill and I have presented dozens of Gift Community seminars in England, France and throughout the US; from Portland to Raleigh, from Santa Barbara to Manhattan.

We are at an auspicious time in history. Structures are breaking down, disciplines long held are up for renewal and paradigms that have held for thousands of years are in the midst of profound change. We as humans feel all of this and a deep need for a place of belonging. We Need Each Other invites you on a journey to create your own community as we step into the emerging Gift Culture.

Chapter 5   Bonding vs. Bridging:
An important Distinction

__Bonding__ catalyzes potency, which catalyzes __bridging__.

Understanding the difference between "bonding" and "bridging" social capital is important as we imagine building core community. Because this book is all about bonding communities, this distinction will allow us to focus attention on exactly what we want so we can clearly see our best possibilities.

As I was searching for a good working definition of community I found a powerful and useful distinction that allowed me to see a unique power in the MKP work over these last 25 years. In his wonderful book with the great title *Community: The Structure of Belonging*, Peter Block mentions Robert Putnam, the author of *Bowling Alone,* one of my all-time favorite classic books. Block points out how Putnam, in his new book *Better Together*, written with Lewis Feldstein, distinguishes between "bonding" and "bridging" social capital.

Putnam and Feldstein explain what *social capital* refers to as they lament the loss of social capital:
>"social networks, norms of reciprocity, mutual assistance, and
>trustworthiness. The central insight of this approach is that social networks
>have real value both for the people in those networks, as well as for
>bystanders."
>"…our stock of—the very fabric of our connections with each other—has
>plummeted, impoverishing our lives and communities."

They continue with the clear distinction:
>"Bonding social capital are networks that are inward looking, composed of
>people of like mind." Bridging social capital networks "encompass
>different types of people and tend to be outward looking."

Peter Block uses the distinction to make it clear that his book focuses on bridging communities. **This book you are reading is all about bonding communities.** Both ways of rebuilding the social capital, that has been lost, feel deeply important at this time in the world.

Most of the social capital building we see locally and around the world is of the bridging variety. As Paul Hawken noted in his visionary book *Blessed Unrest: How the Largest Movement in the World Came into Being*:

> "I soon realized that my initial estimate of 100,000 organizations was off by at least a factor of ten, and I now believe there are over one – and maybe even two – million organizations working toward ecological sustainability and social justice."

While I profoundly honor and support these magnificent bridging projects, the communities I envision are of the *bonding* variety. For 25 years I have observed closely how so many men of MKP bond in their I-groups. Rooted in these friendship communities, they often find the energy and volition to "live their mission," which leads to deeply impactful and wonderful *bridging* community projects. These small groups of men supporting each other have generated thousands of splendid "social inventions" serving children, women, minorities, the disabled, the incarcerated, and other people around the world.

Every year, for over ten years, MKP has given out the annual Ron Hering Mission of Service awards. The men from each of the forty centers choose one man who has manifested his mission in a particularly remarkable way. Every year as I see these men blessed for the beautiful service projects they lovingly have guided into our world. It always touches my heart and I feel so proud of my brothers. Men in loving bonded groups find their hearts and the motivation to do bridging work in the world.

In this context I hold this vision for bonding communities to amp up the size and power of the gifts. If a bonded group of five to ten members such as the MKP I-groups can generate so many positive projects and changes, imagine the potential of a bonded community of 30-150 men and women joyously supporting each other.

Now imagine hundreds of core gift community groups living harmoniously with others. It's a potent vision for our future. Bonding generates trust. Trust provides the footings that creative projects require. From this base we can easily see these communities creating safety nets for each other, including food, healthy medical care, education, even a complementary currency system that keeps wealth local.

By expanding our capacity to trust and being trustworthy, we further our ability to build bridges between divisions in the larger world.

Chapter 6   A Social Movement

"Social movements are humanity's immune response to political corruption, economic disease, and ecological degradation."

Paul Hawken

"I don't know of any great movement that hasn't depended on base communities to sustain individuals in the demanding work of social change."

Parker Palmer

Parker Palmer, a very wise and courageous truth-teller I have admired for decades, precedes the above quote with this observation:

> "[I]nstitutional change doesn't come about simply through the actions of courageous whistle-blowers. **It happens through the formation of communities of people who have a shared moral concern and who can provide encouragement, resources, and protection for each other.**"

Duane Elgin, in his 2010 edition of *Voluntary Simplicity,* calls for "a new village movement" or "greenhouses of human invention." Indeed, right now the world needs social artists, architects and inventors all humming along—full speed imagining, building and disseminating the social designs of the new culture. In Gift Community our task is to provide the fertile soil in which new methods can grow. In joy we water and nurture the buds regularly, keep them warm, harvest when ready, and launch into the larger neighborhood, community and eventually into the world.

The movement of social inventors has begun in earnest. We use different names for these change agents—for example, the **social artists** of Jean Houston, the **social entrepreneurs** of David Gershon and the **social architects** of Jim Channon. By whatever name, each invites us to offer our creative gifts as we step up to do what needs to be done.

Jean Houston, my friend and fellow resident of Ashland, Oregon, calls us Social Artists because we are creating it fresh as we go. We have no map, just a feel for the beauty that is possible. "Social Artistry," she has written, "is the art of enhancing human capacities in the light of social complexity. It seeks to bring new ways of thinking, being and doing to social challenges in the world." It was her old friend Margaret Mead who famously said, "Never doubt that a thoughtful group of committed citizens can change the world. Indeed, it is the only thing that ever has."

David Gershon, in his visionary new book *Social Change 2.0: A Blueprint for Reinventing Our World,* says, "Given the scale of change required to pull our planet back from the brink we need a social entrepreneurship revolution. To do this we need to increase the percentage of people who walk this path from one in a thousand to ten or even a hundred in a thousand."

Jim Channon suggests that social inventions can be most anything created by humans, however social architectures focus on culturally significant purposeful creation. He says, "The purpose of social architecture is to make known the tools and practices for the conscious construction of a planetary civilization."

The following examples of social inventions on his website are focused on youth; they are but a sample of the volume of ideas and practices that cross all social distinctions:

> **Bamboo Rites of Passage**: Young males plant bamboo stands instead of shooting small birds as a rite of passage that, by on their 21st birthday, will produce material for a house, all its furniture, and the necessary household implements.
> **The Learning Village:** Middle schools and high schools open their campuses to elders with real world knowledge and the simulations of work so necessary to practice real skills.
> **The Rollerblade Forest:** A high-mix permaculture forest is interlaced with rollerblading paths. Young people plant and harvest the forest, using starts developed at the intergenerational seed bank.
> **Animal Shrines:** Youth and national guard teams create animal habitats using food, water, nesting, and complementary wildlife.

You may be the social inventor your friends are waiting for. **Your core community could be one of these new social inventions.** This movement starts with your vision, intention and the next conversation.

Chapter 7   Dark Times: A Little Faster Now

"In dark times there is a tendency to gather together."

Michael Meade

In this chapter we will explore the consequences of the old stories of "infinite growth on a finite planet" and "humans own the earth." These assumptions of human exceptionalism have taken civilization inevitably to the brink of the scary word "collapse."

Many of us sense that civilization as we have known it is changing is some dramatic ways; our economic, energy and environmental systems are losing their ability to support us in the ways we have always known. If we are paying attention at all, we must wonder how these will affect us, and what can we do. Indeed, collapse is slowly happening every day as these systems crumble little by little over years. As Carolyn Baker puts it,

> "I believe that collapse will look more like rolling down a hill than falling from a cliff, but some bumps in the roll down the hill will be more painful than others, and with each succeeding bump, it will be clearer that words like 'sea change' and 'point of no return' are the only appropriate synonyms for our experience."

The build-up to the "crash" of 1929 took years. Interestingly, the people who lived through the Great Depression often say that they were not fully aware of it until afterwards. It can be difficult to appreciate the enormity of events while they are happening. The changes that we face today are a more complex perfect storm of economic, energy, and environmental disintegration all at the same time.

This collapse, which some graciously refer to as "The End Of The World As We Knew It," is global and we are all in this together. We are all being affected as the ecological systems of life continue diminishing. The oceans are declining due to plankton loss in the food chain and over-fishing. Our food systems are waning as topsoil depletion causes loss in total world grain production. And the decline of cheap energy, on which our entire civilization is based, has begun as our global population keeps growing.

Many of us already feel old systems dissolving on a personal level as the economic meltdown touches us. As Carolyn Myss states in the introduction to Andrew Harvey's new book called *The Hope*:

"Our present cycle of change has come with new challenges so great that we are incapable of calculating all of them, much less comprehending the interconnected web of catastrophes the challenges portend. How can we comprehend or even imagine what tomorrow will bring? And I do mean tomorrow, as in 'the next day.' Already we have seen the monetary system collapse in a matter of days, something no one believed possible. But as we are learning, nothing is the same as it was even last year. We are, all of us, now headed into a very different world.

"I've come to understand that aside from the obvious social, political, economic, and environmental challenges facing us, there are even more treacherous subtle forces at play. I consider them even more treacherous because we pay them no mind, yet they are reshaping us like silly putty. Specifically, I am aware of how change is increasingly rapid. We cannot calculate how fast business, money, nations, politics, ideas, and laws—essentially anything and everything—changes. We can't keep up anymore, not with our families, not with our friends, and certainly not with ourselves. And of all the things in life we fear most, change is at the top of the list. So here we are living in a world, which is essentially out of control at light speed. Yet no one is addressing this fact, much less the emotional, psychic, mental or physical consequences of this crisis."

Carolyn goes on to say that every change is global in magnitude (like the worker solidarity of Egypt and Wisconsin) and all changes are laden with significance well beyond our ability to grasp, leaving us on continual overload. Over the months I've been writing this book, nearly every day something significant shows up and I say "Oh, I've got to include that." Finally, I decided to stick to the basics of gift community and trust you to keep current as best you can. In the index, I've included some of my favorite websites, which in my judgment tell the highest level truth I can find, and just a couple of important informational sites.

My friend the prolific author John Michael Greer frames our current situation by using the distinction between a problem and a predicament. He points out that a problem is something that calls for a solution, whereas a predicament has no solution, it must be lived out. He then suggests with his great earthy compassion *"that predicaments don't stop being predicaments just because we treat them as problems."* Greer advises us to face squarely our current predicament in all its complexity.

"So many of us want things all one way or the other, all good or all evil, without the terrible ambivalence that pulses through all things human as inescapably as blood. So many of us want to see today's civilization as

26

humanity's only hope or as ecocide incarnate, and long for a future that will be either the apotheosis or the final refutation of the present. It's far less popular, and arguably far more difficult, to embrace that ambivalence and accept both the wonder and the immense tragedy of our time. Still, it seems to me that if we are to face up to the challenges of the future that's bearing down on us, that difficult realization is an essential starting point."

If we hold the "ambivalence" that Greer mentions we may be able to see beyond the speed of change and inevitable collapse. Perhaps there is a balance needed here between examining the obvious dangers we face and appreciating the enormous resources we have available to address our predicament. Ted Nordhaus and Michael Shellenberger, from their book, *BREAK THROUGH: From the Death of Environmentalism to the Politics of Possibility*: suggest that to make change we must focus on building a politics of shared hope rather than fear.

> "Cautionary tales and narratives of eco-apocalypse tend to provoke fatalism, conservatism, and survivalism among voters—not the rational embrace of environmental policies. This research is consistent with extensive social-science research that strongly correlates fear, rising insecurity, and pessimism about the future with resistance to change.
> In promoting the inconvenient truth that humans must limit their consumption and sacrifice their way of life to prevent the world from ending, environmentalists are not only promoting a solution that won't work, they've discouraged Americans from seeing the big solutions at all. For Americans to be future-oriented, generous, and expansive in their thinking, they must **feel secure, wealthy, and strong.**"

I believe that this is where authentic community can make all the difference. With the support of our community we may come to "feel secure, wealthy, and strong." Thus we sustain expansive thinking as we both find hope of abundance shared and relax into an opportunity to live more simply. In this paradoxical way we very well may find a life richer than we had dared to imagine.

"Soul has lived through dark times before."

Michael Meade

Chapter 8   New Story: We Need Each Other

"The most important question facing humanity is this: Can we reach global empathy in time to avoid the collapse of civilization and save the earth?"

Jeremy Rifkin

Gaia is ailing and we are the immune system! This is my favorite new story simply because it reflects the "magic" that is showing up all around Mother Earth. We cannot live separate from her. We need her! We need each other! We are her children, her lovers, and her protectors. We intuitively know that we must devote our lives to healing her or we will die. *We Need Each Other* **is the new story.**

Visionary environmental activist Paul Hawken truly gets Gaia's pain. As he traveled all over the world teaching, people kept coming up to him after his presentations and giving him cards about what they were doing. After several years and thousands of cards, he realized there is something going on here on planet earth that is deep but quiet and gets no press. So he wrote *Blessed Unrest: How the Largest Movement in the World Came into Being and Why No One Saw It Coming* about the healing he sees going on everywhere.

In spring of 2009, in his University of Portland commencement address, Paul addressed our paradox with an encouraging observation:

> When asked if I am pessimistic or optimistic about the future, my answer is
> always the same: If you look at the science about what is happening on
> earth and aren't pessimistic, you don't understand data. But if you meet the
> people who are working to restore this earth and the lives of the poor, and
> you aren't optimistic, you haven't got a pulse. What I see everywhere in the
> world are ordinary people willing to confront despair, power, and
> incalculable odds in order to restore some semblance of grace, justice, and
> beauty to this world.

He offered a quote from the poet Adrienne Rich: "'So much has been destroyed I have cast my lot with those who, age after age, perversely, with no extraordinary power, reconstitute the world.'" Then he commented,

> There could be no better description. Humanity is coalescing. It is
> reconstituting the world, and the action is taking place in schoolrooms,
> farms, jungles, villages, campuses, companies, refugee camps, deserts,

fisheries, and slums. You join a multitude of caring people. No one knows how many groups and organizations are working on the most salient issues of our day: climate change, poverty, peace, deforestation, water, hunger, conservation, human rights, and more. This is the largest movement the world has ever seen. Rather than control, it seeks connection. Rather than dominance, it strives to disperse concentrations of power.

This hope in the face of danger is reflected as Richard Heinberg says "It is a scary time to be alive, but it is a wonderful time to be alive. It is good to know that there is so much accumulated intelligence and compassion among us." And, recently:

> Even though the collapse of the world's financial and industrial systems has started, effort now at minimizing further dire consequences is essential. Collapse does not mean extinction. A new way of life will almost certainly emerge from the wreckage of the fossil-fueled growth era. It is up to those of us who have some understanding of what is happening, and why, to help design that new way of life so that it will be sustainable, equitable, and fulfilling for all concerned. We all need practical strategies and tools to weather the collapse and to build the foundation of whatever is to come after.

Indeed this book, *We Need Each Other*, is carefully designed as one of the "practical strategies and tools" as we peer into the future. There is also amazing hope if we look for it and can stretch into feeling "secure, wealthy, and strong" as alluded to in the previous chapter.

Very recently, I've encountered a new friend and visionary, Timothy Nobles, who advances a "radical hope thesis"—he says "we as a species are wise, wealthy, and competent beyond our current belief or comprehension." He has shared with me some draft chapters from his forthcoming book, *Growing Up as A Species: Our Transition to Sustainable Abundance* in which he offers a radically different perspective on "collapse":

> In the past sixty years, the global material wealth and competence of our species has increased beyond our ability to comprehend its magnitude and implications. But, boom and bust economic cycles and the sense that our economic agreement is a shaky house of cards that could collapse at any moment have resulted in a pervading fear that keeps us from seeing and realizing how enormously wealthy and competent we as a species have become.

It's true that our current economic agreement is a shaky house of cards, but it is sitting on a wide and deep base. This base consists of billions of smart, educated, connected, enterprising people who are equipped with an astounding array of powerful communication and coordination tools and who have easy access to vast information resources. This base could erect a new and much sounder economic agreement within a matter of days.

In response to the question, "If we're so wealthy, why do we feel poor?" he says,

> Why does it seem like there's not enough? In modern industrial economies, most of our hours of work and most of our material resources are used to feed the unproductive churning of our convoluted economic and governmental infrastructures rather than to feed and support people. This unproductive churning is all about attempting to protect ourselves from each other, which just creates more conflict and more need for protection. Our fear-based modes of interacting, organizing, and educating are suppressing or diverting most of the energy, creativity, and productivity of our people. On both personal and societal levels, our energy is diverted from productive support of life and used instead in activities of attack, defense, control, and mass distraction.

How to stop this tragic waste of our money, our energy, and our joy? Timothy proposes a strategy for rapidly triggering a global "quantum leap in trust." One element of that strategy that appeals to my heart is encouraging "communities of trust and abundance" that network globally. Another element is a plan to create a global consensus to fully implement the strategies laid out by our leading experts to quickly eliminate deadly poverty and to launch worldwide effective programs to stop destroying and begin restoring the earth's life support systems.

These strategies have been brilliantly described in best-selling books: *The End of Poverty*, by Dr. Jeffrey Sachs, who is the originator of the field of developmental economics, and in *Plan B 4.0: Mobilizing to Save Civilization* by Lester Brown, legendary founder of the World Watch Institute and author of over fifty books on conserving the resources of the earth. Both authors estimate that their goals could be attained with a carefully targeted investment of just under $200 billion annually. Timothy notes that $200 billion is about *one twentieth of one day's volume of currency trading* on the FOREX foreign exchange market. Also, it is less than one third of one percent of our current global GDP of $70 trillion dollars.

PART 2

COMMUNITY

"By community,
I mean the commonwealth and common interests, commonly
understood, of people living together in a place and wishing to
continue to do so.
To put it another way, community is a locally understood
interdependence of local people, local culture,
locally economy and local nature."

Wendell Berry

Chapter 9   What is Community? A Definition

Because there are so many types of community—neighborhood, work, sports, church, and associations—getting a simple definition can be challenging. We will look beyond the poetic classics, such as Wendell Berry's, to explore more precise definitions of authors Carolyn Schaffer and Pat Murphy.

My friend Carolyn Schaffer, co-author of *Creating Community Anywhere: Finding Support and Connecting in a Fragmented World,* suggests that her definition strives to broadly context community and "contains a time factor and encompasses both traditional forms and the newer ones of social pioneers."
"Community is a dynamic whole that emerges when a group of people
1. Participate in common practices;
2. Depend on one another;
3. Make decisions together;
4. Identify themselves as part of something larger than the sum of their individual relationships;
5. Commit themselves for the long term to their own, one another's and the group's well being."

If we put these features into a single sentence, we arrive at this definition:
Community is a dynamic whole that emerges when a group of people **share** *common practices;* **depend** *on one another;* **make decisions** *together;* **identify** *themselves as part of something larger than the sum of their individual relationships, and* **commit** *themselves for the long term to their own, one another's, and the group's well being.*

Schaffer goes on to note that certain timeless qualities epitomize every type of community, whether they are traditional or newly emerging. Chief among these qualities is commitment. Be it to a group, to family, place, clear communications, or the healthy working out of conflict, it will require that members embody certain values such as trust, honesty, compassion, and respect.

Pat Murphy, co-founder of Community Solutions and author of the recently published *Plan C: Community Survival Strategies for Peak Oil and Climate Change,* defines community as "a group of people attached to a particular place with common interests concerning the issues of their shared place. In other words, communities are people with common interests living in a particular area, an interdependent population of various kinds of individuals in a common location. Often communities are defined as place based, a useful phrase. Such communities of place have been the norm for all of human history."

It's significant that Murphy mentions **"place"** six times in his short definition. There is a reason why, which we will explore in Chapter 35.

A Story about Indigenous Community

A few weeks ago I received an e-mail with a story from my friend Dr. Jack Travis, who founded the Wellness Movement in the 1970s. He had just returned from an anti-circumcision teaching trip to South Africa. Because I've been to South Africa three times and visited a similar township, I deeply felt the truth of his words.

"On my second to last day, Daniel and I drove up the coast to a San people's education center and museum [aka bushmen—remember "The Gods Must Be Crazy"?] where we got a taste of their former life. We even learned their six different click sounds." "On the last day I toured the black township of Langa with a friend of a wellness consultant I just met while there. Our tour guide actually lives in the township. Some might call these "townships" slums but they are pockets of real community—the tour was the high point of my trip—seeing so many happy bonded people (it was a sunny Sunday morning). Our guide took us to her home and some friends' homes (7 people in one bedroom!). But it confirmed for me that the currency of wellness IS connection. These people have a connection with themselves and each other in a way we white folk can barely imagine. And we aren't ever gonna get it through materialistic pursuits."

Chapter 10   Types of Community

This book proposes a specific form of "core" community. So, by way of contrast, it might be useful to do a brief review of various old and new types of community And some wonderful emerging experiments, especially "Gift Circles."

Accidental Communities: These happen as gatherings of whoever shows up in city block, church, office, softball team, night classes, or in a suburban housing development. Accidental groupings have been the way most connections we call "community" happen in current culture.

Intentional Communities: These are groups of people who have chosen to live together with a common purpose. They work cooperatively to create a lifestyle that reflects their shared core values. There have been many religious experiments like the Amish, and the Shakers over the last couple hundred years in which membership required living together in community. Some flourished, and others ended. In the 1960s many creative communes like The Farm in Tennessee emerged. Some survived, others faded. More recently there has been a movement toward ecovillages and co-housing with an emphasis toward elder co-housing.

Community Gardens and Yard Sharing: These are about both connection and resource sharing. Many people have become aware that their yards can be much more than grass, and there are simple things that make a difference. Sharing a home garden is a way for a neighborhood community to empower itself, for people to grow. If a person owns a home and has space for a garden, he can gift some of that space to another person who has time to create the garden. In return, the homeowner can get a share of the food. Production beyond what the gardener and property owner cannot consume can be donated.

Common Security Clubs: This is an innovation that has sprung up in more than 50 cities since 2009 in response to the collapsing economy. Such clubs have been described as "reality support groups" because their members unflinchingly look at the signs of the times. The clubs have moved past their original goal of simply weathering the crisis and have begun to work toward reforms—both local and national—that would prevent a repeat of the devastation.

Virtual community: These non-face-to-face social networks are made up of individuals who interact through media crossing most traditional boundaries. People on sites like Facebook and Twitter share some mutual interests or goals.

The Gift Circle:

In 2009 we held a four-day training called Seeding the Gift Culture at a retreat center outside of Ashland. Fifteen women and fifteen men attended. The event catalyzed great learning for all of us as we experienced tribe stretching into deeper comprehension of gifting potential. After the event we began to meet monthly and stayed in touch around the country. We were bursting with the seeds that had been planted together. And we were strengthened as we practiced being the gift.

We were delighted to learn that one of the men who attended the retreat, Alpha Lo, co-author of *Open Source Collaboration,* distilled the experience into a social invention he dubbed the "Gift Circle." People gather each week and take the time to go around the circle and let each one say what they want or need, such as house cleaning, dog walking, tutoring or a ride to the airport. This allows the others to give a gift to meet the unique need. As Alpha's group of people in their 20s to 30s connected week after week then began to form a solid community in the SF Bay area. Inspired by Alpha, Aumatma Shah, another one of the original group, began hosting a gift circle in Berkley. A year later, they have now spread to the Midwest and East coast and a version of the Gift Circle Book is now out and published. http://www.lulu.com/product/paperback/giftcirclebook/13228169

In Ashland we have been holding monthly Gift Circles for over a year. We always begin with a pot-luck meal for connection and camaraderie. Then we circle up and begin the process. Going around the gift circle saying what we need has ignited a wonderful abundance of exchange. The riches of time and services offered range from window washing to book editing, from singing lessons to bereavement counseling. Our friend Jack Leishman has held point guiding the process and we have helped by hosting. Feeling inspired, Jack also gathered people in the healing professions and developed the Gifting Tree Wellness Center as a "gift clinic."

The gift circle is a brilliant way to introduce concepts of gift culture without the constraints of commitments. One reason it works to bond people is that they get together to actually do something outside of the group meetings. These gift circles also offer a comfortable way to become familiar with people we are considering for core gift community. Our gift circle is becoming so popular that a larger venue will soon be needed. We have also discovered that, for many of us, gifting is easier than receiving. So, it's a great place to practice receiving.

Connecting with neighbors: Beginning with the people next door or down the street seems like such an obvious start. But can it work? Our friend Nik sent the letter below to 35 neighbors in a spread-out rural neighborhood:

Dear Neighbors:

Some have asked what to expect at the January 23rd social at Bob and Janice's house from 1 to 4pm.

First off, we are not going to talk about road repair or dogs. Let's take a few hours to get to know one another and enjoy the sweets of our labors.

If our economy is on the mend, and we all hope it is, then we can sigh a breath of relief, relax a little and simply enjoy our time together, but, if the economy continues along the same path or worsens, then knowing one another might just be the difference we will need to help see all of us through these times.

Things to Bring:

#1. A delectable dessert or finger food to share with your neighbors.

#2. Think about a skill, knowledge or service you might have to offer our immediate neighborhood. Something you will enjoy giving. As an example, a person might love to take care of horses or dogs or children. There might be a plumber in our midst. Someone else might be good with computers, while another has a passion for cooking. Maybe someone has a patch of land that gets lots of sun for the community to build a garden. Someone might have a tractor or rototiller to prepare that garden.

See you there,

Nik

Why this event succeeded had to do with the structure and intent. Nik established a safe place where each person could share her strengths and be heard without it turning in rehashing of disputes over fence lines and dogs. To do this, he waited until everyone was introduced and settled, then people were asked to pair up with someone they did not know. Each person was then given two minutes speak about what he did and enjoyed giving. Nik rang a chime and the pairs switched roles. Then they reformed the circle and each person had two minutes to introduce her partner and say what his gift or passion was. For a number of people their grandchildren was what they enjoyed, but many other very personal exchanges came out of this encounter. Because "check-in" was timed, people actually were appreciated and listened to each other, which created a level of harmony and networking. The gathering will happen again soon. Meanwhile, it has improved cooperation and connection in the neighborhood.

Chapter 11   How Community Feels

"After dinner you sit with some tea and reflect on the evening. Maybe you talk with others about the people in the world who are hungry and how lucky you are to have good food; or maybe you sit quietly, watching people smile and laugh, and you remember stews that your mother cooked and the good times you had with your family and how glad you are that you keep in close touch with friends and family. You feel grateful that you've given up your hectic lifestyle and switched to a less demanding job. In the past you would never have enjoyed cooking a stew. But now serving food to your friends has a new significance. This is what it's all about, you think as you listen to the laughter: the gathering with friends and creating community."

Cecile Andrews

Below is a simple vision of how a weekly meeting might develop and feel when we get together. Notice how we go SLOWLY!

Imagine: On Sunday afternoon we gently show up around 3:30 to 4:00. We slowly greet friends, feeling safe and welcome. We enjoy the warmth of cherishing and belonging with these people. As we move around, sharing with these precious friends, others are preparing the weekly feast.

At 5:30ish we sit together in small groups and share our meal (often pot luck, sometimes food we've cooked together). Perhaps special dishes prepared with love for those near and dear will be presented and honored as to content and intent. We relish continued personal conversation and laughter, which is more fun with each passing month and year.

By 6:15 we focus our attention on the group and listen to each other. Sometimes there may be a personal "check-in" and other times a presentation (perhaps music or theater games), shared contemplative silence, or a discussion of current social or political conditions. The circle becomes a place in which everyone "shines" at one time or another; we take turns offering our personal gifts. Each gathering has a unique yet consistent flavor.

By 8:00ish we are complete, say our "good-byes," and return to our individual homes, each feeling that warm sense of love and belonging. We each know our shared community and ourselves just a bit deeper.

The Benefits And Blessings Received

Together we grow social capital—we might just call it intimacy. Because we know each other's situations, passions, and work in the world, we are always eager for up-dates on how they're going. These might be given in the one-to-one conversations, the spontaneous groupings, intentional small groups, or even in formal presentations. The trust grows because the support is constant and enveloping. And so it builds, each word shared, each hour spent together working, playing, sometimes grieving, sometimes celebrating. We become a distinct community, which gathers regularly and often to share food as well as social, spiritual, and political awareness. Each member takes responsibility as we work together to create the community we want and cherish.

Real Life Example

We had the most splendid liminal birthday party one magnificent evening last April. On this particular birthday, Zoe would become the same age at which her dad had died. She had big inner resistance to being that exact age, so we kept putting off calling friends for a birthday gathering. Finally, with just two days left, she knew what she needed. We called friends, who accepted. Eight of her women friends took her up to the creek for a dip into the water as a ritual cleansing. It involved setting intention, a ritual purification with smudge and marking paints. Emerging from her icy plunge, she was received in towels and blankets held by her friends. Two of the other women also took the opportunity to go into the water for their own intentions as the others assisted with joy and loving support.

Meanwhile, back home the men intuitively knew what to do. Even though late in the afternoon we had only the vaguest idea of a ritual or ceremony, we know how to work together, trusting each other's gifts. Once together and cooking, the process evolved organically. A plan and flow of the evening quickly came clear. "I know how to cook;" "I used to be a waiter, I'll take the orders;" "I'll take point on the ritual parts." We joyously prepared the "pot-luck" hot soups, sweet cakes, and other courses to serve and care for our goddesses upon their return.

When they arrived, we greeted the women at the door with an arch of arms of welcome and honoring. We gently guided them into the living room area made comfortable with cushions and pillows. Once settled, we offered a drink—water, tea, or wine—and served what each chose.

When time came for the meal, our ritual master invited everyone to stand for a prayer of gratitude and honoring the birthday guest. Soon we began serving the salad. The pot-luck meal had provided two options, and since the waiter had taken the orders, everyone received just what she wanted. The men joined in the meal, many sitting on the floor at the women's feet. As we cleared the salad plates, we took orders for the soup (Indian dahl or organic chicken veggie). Again we sat with everyone sipping our soup.

Then came time for the birthday blessing ritual. The floor was opened for anyone to share personal appreciations with Zoe. Warm words of love flowed over Zoe, and it was her task simply to receive. When the time felt right, one of the women picked up a guitar, which was close at hand, and began to sing easy songs that drew us all into the musical flow at that moment.

As the musical energy waned, the men offered desserts from three options (ricotta cheese cake, wheat flour-free chocolate brownies, and blackberry cobbler), which we brought around and served as each requested. I got to follow the servers, squirting organic whipped cream on whatever dessert delight she had chosen, or sometimes all three.

It was all very joyous and effortless. We know how to do these things. We know how to trust the process and our collective ability to know what to do and how to do it. There was no leader as such. We have faith that a task leader will step up as needed to do his giving, then return into the group to enjoy receiving. We give and receive with equal delight. Some of us men have been preparing for decades to meet women who tend to do all this so much more naturally than we.

So we're writing this experience into this book both to acknowledge our readiness and to illustrate how gifting can work wonderfully.

Chapter 12   A Safety Net for a New Generation

"If we wish to survive the social and ecological crisis that we have created we need to get deeply involved in the development of new community structures within our society."

Lynn Margulis

Prolific visionary author Parker Palmer says, "Rebuilding is going to require lots of Americans to re-envision what abundance means." He tells of his feeling more abundance in a Quaker community living on $2,400 a year plus room and board, than he had at many other times of his life. He suggests,

> "This abundance comes from knowing that we're there for one another. If the bottom falls out of my life, I have a support net and if the bottom falls out of your life, I can be part of the support net for you. That's abundance."

There appears to be more and more reason to suggest that we have come to the end of the age of abundance. The deepwater Gulf of Mexico oil gusher may be the wake-up call. In the light of peak oil, the magical thinking of infinite growth is being recognized. The way of life we had assumed would last forever is being seen more realistically now. Most of us will be poorer; some will worry about getting enough food or adequate medical care; many will not have the opportunity to retire; nor will we have the security of having police and firefighters always on call. All these things that we take for granted are becoming more problematic.

The changes we are witnessing do not mean a future of never-ending misery. Difficult times have happened before. In the United States the most recent long, hard decline to hit Western societies was the Great Depression, which began in 1914 and lasted until eventually the "war economy" caused prosperity to return to the land. Well before that time, in the later part of the 1800s, men and their families were leaving the farms and coming into cities, often to work in the newly developing factories and mines which at the beginning of industrial civilization. These changes led to a predicament.

Before any government regulation or unions, men would often get killed on the job and there was no one to care for their families. Spontaneously, "fraternal orders" arose to function as safety nets to protect their members' families. They were known simply as "lodges," and people embraced these communities. Self- created and sustained, the lodges served well until the wealth of the country and liberal policies of government created programs of social security to protect citizens.

Because the fraternal orders were no longer needed for their original function, they reconfigured as benevolent organizations with a "men's night out" social function.

Today, we are increasingly coming to know the need once again for such a safety net. We see our governments as being increasingly incapable of caring for citizens. The reasons for this are complex political and economic, but we can already see the need for "safety nets" as a way to care for each other. The well-tested "lodge" process worked for many decades, and this book reflects some of the wisdom from that model.

There is a great deal of information available on preparations for hard times, such as storing food, garnering resources, and providing one's own protection. The social and inner preparation, however, is more significant than anything material we can do. We intend to take you deep into understanding how you might create your own community as the safety net for your family and many others in your community. In this way we can consciously cultivate our inner resources and internal resilience.

We have been telling the people that this is the Eleventh Hour
Now you must go back and tell the people that this is the Hour
And there are things to be considered
Where are you living?
What are you doing?
What are your relationships?
It is time to speak your truth
Create your community.
The time of the lone wolf is over, Gather yourselves!

Message from the Hopi Elders

Chapter 13   Tribe of Choice

We are all bundles of potential that manifest only in relationship. Thus, when we're in good relationships, based on a generosity of spirit and not 'what's in it for me' we discover new potentials and create new potentials together. The narrow sense of self, where we focus only on our needs, keeps us and all from realizing new potentials. So life is all about relationships which then gift us with new discoveries. Being in good relationships is the only way to release this energy of life, which always wants to move toward the new and does so with great flair and abundance.

Margaret Wheatley

As suggested earlier in the book, the tribe, not the family is our basic social unit. We may feel attracted to a "family of choice," but what we are really going for in this book is literally choosing our "tribe."   This is why we hold 30-150 as an ancient functional tribal number.

You can take people out of the tribe, but you cannot take tribe out of people. The first communities of humans were not families, but tribes. The human family is embedded in tribal community. The tribe is an integral part of our human social existence that lies beyond recorded history. It is archetypal and it lives in us all. For most of human history we have been tribal beings, and as such knew our "selves" as tribe, not as separate identities.

Within the last few centuries a separate "self" identity emerged, which in its separateness could feel the constraint or constriction of others and decided to choose to act separately from tribe. This differentiation needed to happen, yet the individual became more and more individualized, perhaps far beyond "enough" autonomy. Isolation and alienation became normal.

Just in our lifetime we have seen human community dissolve and leave people bereft of their inner morality and sense of responsibility. People were torn away from organic communities. Piece by piece, this also separated them from their own inner essence or soul.

In his brilliant writing on tribal community culture, Dr. Dieter Duhm is very clear about how essential community is to our healthy development as humans:

"Community was and is the natural breeding ground for trust and solidarity. . . . Community is an intermediate stage in the scale of life, and it cannot be skipped. It connects the individual with a higher order and sharpens her/his sense of the whole. A healthy community reflects a universal order, with which we can then connect easier. It is through this connection that a functioning community gets its high field-creating power."

It seems obvious that we need to re-tribe, but we cannot simply go back because we are so very different from old style tribal ancestors. And we can't learn much from tribes because, as author John Robb points out,

"[L]ike most people in the so-called developed world, you have little experience in a true tribal organization. Tribal organizations have been systematically crushed in the last couple of centuries, both by the dominant nation-states that saw them as competitors, and by the marketplace that saw them as impediments. Tribal people tend to be self-sufficient and satisfied. It is difficult to politically control, or sell mass-produced products on credit, to people who are self-sufficient and satisfied."

Robb further suggests that development of resilient communities may be rooted in the tribal practice of fictive kinship. He sees this process at work in the Transition Towns movement with their story telling, honoring of elders, re-skilling, and leaderless approach.

The human species needs a new model of living for its existence on planet Earth. There are many emerging possibilities, and I do not know which model is the best (if, indeed, there is any one best model). My job here is pose the right questions and provide relevant information. Our common task is to re-tribalize our culture in a way that is appropriate to who we are today.

PART 3

WHO ARE WE
AND
ARE WE READY?

Rumi says:

***"The cost of loving is your life,
and the lover runs towards him,
handing him a sword,
saying, 'take my head now.'"***

Chapter 14   Adults of God

*"Maybe it's time we children of God finally grow up
and become adults of God, and realize we are
the Creator's creation created to create.
In other words, we're not here to earn God's love,
we're here to spend it!"*   Swami Beyondananda

Are we mature enough? I'm writing this book because I truly believe "adults" are happening, that we are ready for transformation. I believe there are millions who understand the times we live in and that we need each other to respond creatively. We span every race and religion and ethnicity. We are in every country and speak every language.

But just who are we? The people of the new culture whom I have observed have several qualities in common. We are able to look inside and observe our own process and know how we come up with our reality in the moment. We hold values that embrace all of life with respect and honoring, especially around gender equality. With a healthy ego identity, love flows easily. It's all about maturity, about growing up.

Visionary teacher Duane Elgin shares a potent perspective on this, from his own life journey in his book *The Living Universe*:
> "As I traveled around the world giving talks about humanity's future, I
> often began with a simple question: 'When you look at the overall
> behaviors of the human family, what life stage do you think we are in?
> Averaging human behavior around the world, what stage of development
> best describes the human family: toddler, teenager, adult or elder?' When I
> first began asking this question, I had no idea if people would understand it
> and, if they did, how they would answer. To my surprise, nearly everyone
> immediately understood the question and their responses show that, around
> the world, there is an overwhelming agreement about humanity's stage of
> life–we are in our teenage years."

As each individual human grows up, so the world culture grows up. When I was in graduate school in the 1970s, I felt powerfully attracted to the cutting-edge psychological and spiritual opportunities being offered. I experienced the joy of opening to new or hidden parts of myself. And in that same way I followed my passion and became a social pioneer. Now hundreds of thousands of others have

45

been teaching new social, psychological, and spiritual ways for all of us to grow. Millions have been learning and maturing beyond our "teenage" stage.

We have life-affirming principles we live by, and we know how to love each other. We know how much we need each other, and we trust our ability to figure out how to protect and care for each other. Yet, many of us are untested and will not see our own maturity until some specific challenge puts it to work. We will recognize the qualities of leadership that we have already embodied as we begin to make decisions which require greater maturity.

We are pioneers. New ventures, social or otherwise, start with the adventurers, the ones who enjoy moving into new possibilities. Decades ago Arnold Toynbee called such people the "creative minority." More recently, we began to use the terms "early adaptors" or "cultural creatives." This section of the book explores just how these people show up in the world and the qualities that allow them to imagine they can build new community. They are aware of the state of the world and preparing the way. They are pioneering a way of life that is deeply satisfying without requiring massive amounts of energy and "stuff."

"Fulfilled to overflowing" is a beautiful phase from Spiral Dynamics which best describes the new feeling people are embracing. From this knowing of inner peace there is nothing to do but give. **Adults building the gift culture!**

Chapter 15   The "Gift Culture" Movement

"Building a culture of sustainability will require as much creativity, energy, and enthusiasm as we have invested in building cultures of consumption."

Duane Elgin

The Gift Culture movement is a paradigm shift. Its viewpoint is both ancient and modern, cutting through disconnection to our essential nature. It goes beyond the idea of bartering to look at the fundamental nature of our world and universe. It is about discovering gifts we didn't know we had, living in a place of gratitude for life itself, and living in unprecedented trust.

It is very useful to be around people who model this gift culture perspective. One of them is our friend Aumatma Shah, a naturopathic doctor who has been running a "gift clinic" in the San Francisco Bay area for several years. She has been living the "gift" full time and speaks from experience. She suggested the following characteristics of the paradigm shift, which I have developed a bit.

1.   From transaction to trust.   Experiments embodying this shift continue to show up. Obvious examples are clinics like Aumatma's or restaurants without any set amounts on the menu where people pay what the food has been worth to them. The internet has tens of thousands of services that operate by donation. Wikipedia and several other spinoffs operate through gifts of time and creative energy.

Close to our hearts is Burning Man, where we first met and have attended several times. Imagine 50,000 people gathering in the desert for a full week, setting up tents and campers and arts, lots of astonishing art. Especially significant is that at Burning Man there is no commerce whatever, no buying or selling of anything. It's all a gift culture, pure give away. It's all about trust. And this wild experiment has continued for decades.

2.   From consumption to contribution. There is an axiom in the new culture that what people most want is to "give their gift." Another way of saying comes from Joseph Campbell, who famously said "follow your bliss." By bliss he meant joy, which is the experience of becoming a more complex being. With increased complexity something opens up in us that feels good.   This happens when we discover that our gift—some polished skill or talent—serves others in special ways. From gardening to woodwork, music to stonework, cooking to water purification, we all have something to give. And when it is received, the circle of life is complete. We want to give our gift.

A favorite example of ours comes from our friend Katie and her wonderful dog Gelsey. The amazing project is called Dogs for Diabetics. It involves patiently training special dogs to alert diabetic people when their blood sugar levels drop. In this movement o money ever changes hands. The care, patience and nurturing of these exceptional dogs are all pure gift. And the joy and gratitude they bring to people who need this life-giving alert, not to mention warm and cozy side benefits, is reward enough. Everyone wants to give-back.

3. From scarcity to abundance. As we move from a time of the greatest material abundance in human history to a time of impending scarcity, can we redefine abundance and discover it? Indeed we can. There are several keys to this discovery. One is trusting that there is enough to meet everyone's true material needs. A second is the realization that, personally, I may already have enough, thus defying the billions of advertising dollars spent to induce in me a sense of scarcity that can never be satisfied. For example, some gift culture people do not own a TV and have not watched it for more than a decade. These first two keys lead to the third—the realization of our inner abundance. Some people live with an inner abundance expressed by a phrase I used in the previous chapter: "fulfilled to overflowing." Check it out, do you feel fulfilled to overflowing, much of the time? If we try to fill up with food, drinking etc. we feel stuffed, but filled with love, friends and community just plain feels good.

4. From isolation to community. This transition has been the focus of much of my work over three decades. Men in our culture tend to be isolated for so many reasons. In the MKP work, we do what it takes to build trust, to bond and connect men long term with other men on a similar path of inner growth. Each man also creates his own "mission of service" so that he can share his gift in turn. One of our favorite friends, Gordon Clay has lived his personal mission of "ending men's isolation." by sharing his unique gifts for the last 20 years. He developed some amazing trainings that bond men and women very safely in healthy, open-hearted intimacy. He also took his gift virtual with a website (http://www.menstuff.org) to help men connect; it gets several million hits per year.

5. From competition to co-operation. Linux, Wikipedia, Craigslist, Flickr and YouTube are the old timers. Since 2008 the number of "collaborative" programs has mushroomed. Facebook, Freecycle, Swaptree, Couchsurfing and Zipcar are just a few of hundreds of new forms of co-operation. This dramatic movement is called "collaborative consumption". It is often lost on many people in my elder age group because it is so recent. It reflects an inner worldview - very different in younger generations.

In the business world, hierarchal models are giving way to workers' owning the companies and making decisions. In the world of media, the blogs and personal communication are challenging long established newspapers and TV networks. Young people know the emptiness of the old competitive media and are opting for blogs and other alternative information sharing sources. Perhaps most dramatic observation is the "gaming" phenomenon in which half a billion "gamers" play collaboratively with each other all over the world.

In the world of sports I recently discovered Ultimate Frisbee, a sport with nearly a million regular players. There are thousands of teams all over the world that compete regularly, but it is essentially different from normal competition. Cooperation between teams is the rule. Two remarkable things about it stand out for me. First, there are no referees; each player holds an inner integrity called the "spirit of the game" even to the highest levels of advancement. Second, the teams are often mixed gender; men and women play as equals.

So, from Burning Man to Freecycle to Ultimate Frisbee the Gift Culture is showing up everywhere if we have the eyes to see it. Perhaps you are one of the pioneers.

An old saying goes like this: "First they fight you, then they laugh at you, then they say, well it might work, and finally they say I knew it all along . . . in fact it was my idea."

"Hey, you know that gift culture thing, I thought of that years ago."

And just what did you do with your early insight?

Chapter 16   Gift Community

*"The technology we need most is the technology of community –
the knowledge about how to cooperate to get things done.
Our sense of community is in disrepair."*

Bill McKibben

We do not know exactly what a gift community looks like or feels like. Some of us have had experiences for a few hours or even days that might be "it." So we can name it and imagine it and remember some times when we thought we felt it. But honestly, gift community, as best as I have been able to discern it, does not yet exist. This section has several chapters that explore how we might hold and meet the challenge to co-create the core gift community we truly want.

Conversing with visionary writer Charles Eisenstein has been deeply helpful in addressing this challenge. Like me, Charles has traveled from coast to coast and in Europe over the past several years and learned that everyone wants community, an extended family, or tribe. The people we have talked with feel that they do not have what they want and do not have any clear idea how to get it. Charles suggests that they fail in their attempts because they begin from the wrong starting point, one rooted in the old story of our culture. They begin by seeking the community they want, like any other commodity, asking **"What can I get?".**

Charles suggests that a much better starting point, one rooted in the new story, would be asking the question, **"What do I have to give?"** Gift community is about living our gifts, bringing them to others and receiving their gifts in natural reciprocity. Community is about identifying real needs and meeting them together. "What do I have to give?" is the question that leads to community.

Gift community requires the ability and willingness to authentically give and receive. This is one of the essential qualities of the evolving consciousness that this book is calling forth at this moment in history. Our very sense of who we are must evolve in order for us to be able to clearly envision true gift community. Each of us has the capacity to transcend our separate egos and attain a new collective identity. Perhaps this new identity can be described as **our inter-being self,** or **the self of our interconnectedness.** When a group gathers in the spirit of the gift, something new is born. Then miracles are possible.

Chapter 17   Ways of Being Together:
A Four-Stage Map

*There's nothing like an intimate relationship to let us know
that we're not as developed as we thought.*

Robert Augustus Masters

Overview of the four stages: This four-stage relationship map follows human maturation as we grow from infant to adult. Because of our parental and cultural wounding, including our separation from the earth, we may get stuck in a stage we could have grown beyond.

Somewhere from toddler to adolescent we relate from a self-centered identity, an attitude of "What can I get for me?" This is a normal developmental stage, unless the child is very loved. As we mature in our ability to recognize the other as separate and fall in love and feel our needs and attachment we usually bond in what's called co-dependency. Some of us continue to grow emotionally and socially and become more autonomous, self sufficient, differentiated, and individualized. We evolve to an "equal but separate" relationship in which we each have our career, bank account, separate friends, sometimes even separate homes. We love each other, and when we are together it's great. This is actually a highly evolved "way of being." Yet there is still another stage. As an autonomous individual, my identity may become strong enough to consciously allow attachment to another. In this commitment I find an intimacy deep enough to allow transformational process. The "container" of the relationship provides enough safety to accelerate our inner evolution and its outer manifestation. At this stage we feel fulfilled and we feel the need to serve, to give back.

Each of these stages shapes the nature and extent of our participation in community.

The following sections show **what people want** in each stage, **who they are** in the world socially and psychologically, then finally **where** in community they might be found. Each of us can see ourselves living somewhere on this map. It allows us to see ourselves currently in community and imagine how we might want to "be together" with others in the future.

51

FOUR STAGES OF COMMUNITY

I found this wonderful overview of four stages of human intimate relationships developed by Robert Augustus Masters in *Transformation Through Intimacy*. With Robert's permission and support, I've reworked the model as a map showing four stages of community. (For information on his many other books and training events, see http://www.robertmasters.com/)

#1   TOGETHER ALONE: *"I am with people."*
What: People at this stage want to be with other people but not too closely. They may have conversations but don't go very deep. Mostly they talk about things, events, or ideas such as their political opinions.
Who: They usually find trusting other people somewhat challenging. Co-dependent couples or friends will move into these situations together as one, supporting each other in feeling safe with others. Particularly narcissistic types can get attention in such relationships without any commitment.
Where: People find some sense of community through watching sporting events, movies, or going to taverns or political meetings. They are with others, but it is mostly not personal. Their hearts rarely touch.

#2   GLUED TOGETHER: *"I belong to a community."*
What: People at this stage have a strong desire to belong. These folks will give up their own beliefs to be part of a group . To be accepted they will also surrender personal power, money, and freedom.
Who: They show up as needy or co-dependent personality types and are vulnerable to cult-like appeals.
Where: This sense of community can show up in most religions, but it is especially common in fundamentalist religions. A typical promise that "Jesus saves" often translates into, "Once you are one of us, we'll take care of you."

#3   TOGETHER SEPARATELY: *"I am in a community."*
What: Here we find self-sufficient, independent people who want community, particularly with others just like themselves. They have been successful in the outer world and want to share time and co-creative energy with others, so they look for established gatherings of people that they can join.
Who: These folks are detached, high functioning, and individualized. If/when they find others of like mind and shared interest, they join in and slowly develop friendships.
Where: This type of community will show up in main-stream religions and especially in New Thought churches like Unity or Unitarian. Many other kinds of

associations, such as theater groups or political organizations provide similar opportunities.

#4 BEING TOGETHER: *"I am community."*

What: These folks have both healthy autonomy and intimacy skills, including the necessary emotionally openness to be truly present. Being with others in an interdependent way serves their wants and needs for mutual security, support, sustainability, growth, and transformation.

Who: Independent, self-aware, and strong enough to embrace attachment without fear, they voluntarily commit to staying together. They want community that is rather like a good marriage—accessible, not too big or too small, and with a mutual commitment to stay "together." This deep intimacy is the felt essence of "being" community. From this place of fulfilled being there is ease in giving, receiving, and living the gift.

Where: There are place-based communities, such as co-housing and ecovillages, in which these autonomous beings choose to be present together. Beyond such intentional living situations, however, this stage of community appears to be new and untried. Evolving gift communities might just become the new common form.

Chapter 18   Values and Principles

Such human qualities as morality, compassion, decency, wisdom and so forth have been the foundations of all civilizations. These qualities must be cultivated and sustained through systematic moral education in a conductive social environment, so that a more humane world may emerge.
                                                    -His Holiness the Dalai Lama

Historically, community worked well because of shared principles and values. Typically, they came from established religious systems or a charismatic leader or both. Examples can be seen in most fundamentalist religious systems, which hold principles that came directly from their religious leader, God or book. However many of us, who grew up with knowledge available by television and computer, got to observe life from a broader historical and cross-cultural perspective. With these big eyes we could see the obsolete dogma and hypocrisy, making us skeptical of the "one true God" and pre-packaged belief systems. We too often threw out the whole system no matter how popular, ancient or tested. Unfortunately, in those systems were some useful moral guidelines which some of us carried loosely or abandoned.

Many in our generation have struggled well with the challenge to find, hone and embrace clear moral values to guide our lives and our community. In Chap. 31 we explore the principles or values that we feel as most useful in community. It literally took years of testing to sort down to the eight core values that we hold and invite other to share as our core community grows. Zoe and I struggled the most with the issue of spirituality. It seems there are at least ten thousand names for The All That Is, or maybe it is the same hallowed reality understood in myriad ways. We eventually made our "sacred value" very, very inclusive.

Because the champions are the ones who choose these principles their community will share, they face the challenge to make these values appropriate for our times. We want to offer examples of values from organizations we respect as cutting edge experiments in new community. The first is an obvious bias, and I do believe MKP has beautiful values. The other is Burning Man, a twenty-year experiment in Gift Culture. You can feel the deep level of experimentation in their 10 principles.

The ManKind Project Values of the Mature Masculine

Accountability – We do what we say we will do, and don't do what we say we will not do. We take responsibility for our actions, our thoughts and our feelings.

Authenticity – We tell the truth about who we are. We strive to be our best selves.

Compassion – We empathize, connecting to the suffering of others, and we act with love in the world.

Generosity – We recognize that giving of ourselves from our abundance brings more for all. We take on missions of service in the world and work together to make a positive difference.

Integrity – We live our values. We seek wholeness.

Leadership – We step forward in our lives to offer compassionate leadership, seeking understanding and community rather than domination or oppression.

Multicultural Awareness – We recognize that in our world it is imperative that we be able to live in harmony with people who are different than ourselves. We strive to understand ourselves and others and to celebrate our differences.

Respect – We pay attention to the impacts of our actions on others and we treat others with honor.

Ten Principles of Burning Man

Radical Inclusion Anyone may be a part of Burning Man. We welcome and respect the stranger. No prerequisites exist for participation in our community.

Gifting Burning Man is devoted to acts of gift giving. The value of a gift is unconditional. Gifting does not contemplate a return or an exchange for something of equal value.

Decommodification In order to preserve the spirit of gifting, our community seeks to create social environments that are unmediated by commercial sponsorships, transactions, or advertising. We stand ready to protect our culture from such exploitation. We resist the substitution of consumption for participatory experience.

Radical Self-reliance Burning Man encourages the individual to discover, exercise and rely on his or her inner resources.

Radical Self-expression Radical self-expression arises from the unique gifts of the individual. No one other than the individual or a collaborating group can determine its content. It is offered as a gift to others. In this spirit, the giver should respect the rights and liberties of the recipient.

Communal Effort Our community values creative cooperation and collaboration. We strive to produce, promote and protect social networks, public spaces, works of art, and methods of communication that support such interaction.

Civic Responsibility We value civil society. Community members who organize events should assume responsibility for public welfare and endeavor to communicate civic responsibilities to participants. They must also assume responsibility for conducting events in accordance with local, state and federal laws.

Leaving No Trace Our community respects the environment. We are committed to leaving no physical trace of our activities wherever we gather. We clean up after ourselves and endeavor, whenever possible, to leave such places in a better state than when we found them.

Participation Our community is committed to a radically participatory ethic. We believe that transformative change, whether in the individual or in society, can occur only through the medium of deeply personal participation. We achieve being through doing. Everyone is invited to work. Everyone is invited to play. We make the world real through actions that open the heart.

Immediacy Immediate experience is, in many ways, the most important touchstone of value in our culture. We seek to overcome barriers that stand between us and a recognition of our inner selves, the reality of those around us, participation in society, and contact with a natural world exceeding human powers. No idea can substitute for this experience.

Chapter 19   Men and Women Together

Feminism was the most important and powerful evolutionary wave of the twentieth century. Now another wave is rising.

A femininity strong in its sensual and emotional authority. A masculinity confident in its potency and vision.

A masculinity that can truly honor the feminine. A femininity that can truly honor the masculine.

Mark and Elisabeth Josephs-Serra

The masculine needs to connect with its essence. The essence-of-masculine is awesome. On the one hand, it's as still, silent, and vast as the sky; on the other, it's fierce, potent, and passionate. But if the masculine is to unite with the feminine, it MUST connect with this essence-of-itself. Otherwise it just can't handle her. It gets lost in its head and behaves incoherently and, all too often, destructively.

The feminine also needs to connect with its essence. The essence-of-feminine is equally awesome. It's as voluptuous and dangerous as the oceans, and resonant with the deepest mysteries of our dream-lives. Again, to unite with the masculine, the feminine MUST connect with this essence-of-itself. Otherwise it will shrivel back into good-little-girl or rebellious-teenage-girl, disempower itself, collude in one way or another, and betray its most heartfelt knowing.

If we accept these obligations and enter our relationships as sacred journeys of mutual empowerment, then they can return us to our deepest masculinity and femininity. Because this understanding of relationships is so rare, unfamiliar, and difficult, however, we need to create local community that supports such relationships, containers in which couples can support each other.

Mark and Elisabeth Josephs-Serra, authors of the quotations opening this chapter, make it clear that community is imperative to healthy men and women. **As couples we need community, and community needs us. After all, intimate relationship is perhaps the most fundamental and important of all the social structures that sustain community.**

I've been waiting literally for decades for this time when men and women can come together in ways that honor their essential selves. Because my path has been "men's work," I have been aware that men need to do our own inner work, reclaiming of our healthy masculinity, and that this can only be done with other men. As men we need to find our own soul center, that authentic core of who we are. Just like most women, men have been wounded by parents and our culture. These wounds require a safe place for their exploration and healing. That process is a significant part of MKP work.

In my 1992 book *A Circle of Men* I included a chapter, by Danaan Parry a wild creative guy, called "We're Not Ready Yet, But Soon." Parry recounts the time his men's group spent the night on the beach and a related group of women chose to spend the night on the mountain ridge.

> "Separately, we will evoke the energies of our gender: we will try to open to our own, brother to brother, sister to sisters, beyond role and game and expectation. We will try. We will use ritual and dance and story and whatever we can to explore who is this being, man; who is this being, women. And we have talked of what to do in the morning. An agreement— we, the men, will come to the meadow between the ocean shore and the mountain ridge. The women too will come. We will meet, and see what happens. We will try."

Parry goes on to describe his process of opening to what Robert Bly introduced as the "Wildman," the masculine archetype, the deep male subconscious source of primary energy. He told of how he and the men that night with fire and ocean water found the primal energy, reclaimed the feeling of being men without shame. These men knew their power to create, not destroy. It's a great description of men feeling truly free. Eventually,

> "It was time to go to the meadow. We could see the women coming down the trail from the mountain. Images of warm hugs and soft smell were with men now. But as we approached the women, I noticed that my body was beginning to close, just a bit. My shoulders were hunching forward, just a bit. My freely swinging hips were becoming a bit more controlled, more proper. Other noticed their body responses too. We were returning. We were together, men and women, people who care deeply for each other. We were looking at each other, saying nothing. For a long time. One of the women broke the difficult silence. She said, 'Not yet.'
>
> "We all knew what she meant. We turned and walked away. No more words were spoken for many hours. Feelings of sadness and rightness

swept through me. We had touched something during that night, something so deep and vital that for me, man, and her, woman, to attempt to come together *at that level* would have been impossible. For now.

"There will come a time when men and women will come together at that level. But first men, as men, and women, as women, must explore the depths, the incredible depths of who they are. They/we must risk and open and explore and claim the woman-power and the man-power that live in that cave deep within and yet beyond ourselves. We have only just begun."

Parry ends with this:
"Our world cries out for men to move beyond their role-playing and beyond their shame, and to unlock that deep fertile maleness that lives in us. Humankind hungers for this good, grounded male energy, just as surely as it hungers for clear, deep, powerful woman energy. And the integration of those creative forces will birth something very new, very wonderful. Not yet, but soon!"

Bill: I have been waiting for 25 years and I have seen it. We are ready! I have seen men and women together; transparent and safe. I have experienced going beyond my own fears and seductive games into a safe shared intimacy with women that simply feels so deeply good. I believe our generation has been blessed to bring this gift into the world. This is the mature feminine and mature masculine coming together at long last to build intimate community, as it has never been seen before.

Zoe: Yes, we are ready. I, have long been blessed with sisters but over the last decade I now have brothers as well. From these amazing men and women I have learned volumes on how men and women are different. How astonishing it has been to discover that we often use language that has virtually opposite meaning to the other gender. As author Alison Armstrong writes, "Men are not (as women often think) hairy misbehaved women." and women are not, "more lovely, emotionally indulgent men." Misunderstanding has caused much suffering. But the gender differences are being decoded. Our unique needs and gifts can now be understood, appreciated and honored. As we stand in our masculine, in our feminine we have the tools for understanding. We use these insights to empower each other's intrinsic gifts in intimate trusting communities. It is a new day for women and men.

Chapter 20   Loving Each Other

There are two kinds of people, those who have known love and those who haven't.

Paul Newman

Someone asked me not too long ago, "What is the most important thing you have learned about community so far?" I answered, **"Community is you and me."** How simple, yet it has taken me so long to learn this seemingly obvious truth. Because I've been organizing groups for decades, I wanted to "build community" by doing it as a group. That seemed easy enough: call the people together, present the structure, and bingo! instant community. What I was doing fits that classic definition of insanity: Doing the same thing over and over and expecting different results.

Finally I realized that community is profoundly personal! When we get right down to its essence, community is you and me. That's its core. It's about relationships—how you know me and how I know you. Do you trust me? And vice versa.

Then it moves to me and another—let's call him Jeff. How much do I trust Jeff? What communication risks do we take to deepen our trust? Then there is you and Jeff. Where is your trust level with Jeff? Do you feel how complex this is getting? But wait, how about you and Wendy? And what about how I trust Wendy? Now don't forget about Tony, Wendy's husband. That makes four of us now and a spouse. We're getting to be a group. This could lead to community. Sounds good.

Now wait, let's review. It started with you and me, then how we related to Jeff and how we all trusted each other. Then, with Wendy, we seem to have increased our complexity both by adding another person and also the inclusion of her husband raises the personal relationship issue (to say nothing of the challenge of incorporating their children).

This is community building. It's going on all the time. We just seldom notice it. We found that if we simply bring our attention to it, talk about it, and feel the feelings accompanying it, we know what to do and how to do it. Of course any such process entails some risk and requires the courage to address this new level of awareness and truth.

Classically most friendship networks or communities of people develop very slowly and organically. Our best and deepest friends are usually those who we have known for decades. Ten to twenty years is the norm for "good friends" which usually means those who we really trust. We typically meet people in the work place or socially at parenting groups at our kids' school, or maybe at cultural and sporting events. The "getting to know you" process begins slowly and safely, allowing much time for personal distance to be gently transcended. Eventually trust "just happens" and we have an "old friend" (which only took a decade or two). In this era of accelerated change we do not want to wait 20 years.

The MKP organization has taken a different route to build friendships, trust, and community in a far shorter time. It often starts with the trust of one man for another. A guy goes through the training, feels the power of his own open heart. He has a friend who will benefit from the training and become a closer friend. He extends an invitation, and if the trust in their relationship is deep enough, the friends accepts the invitation and risks stepping into a new situation that requires some vulnerability. Once inside, men see and feel something quite different from anything they have known before. Because the situation is safe, hearts open and bonds form in ways participants could never have expected.

This positive experience brings enough security to risk entering into yet another situation that feels even more personal and leads in an amazingly quick way to friendships and even community. These are the I-groups in which men feel supported as they hone their new skills and deepen their inner learning. During the New Warrior Training Adventure weekend, participants live into the new story of healthy masculinity.

The MKP organization has been around for a quarter century now and has served tens of thousand of men. I suggest that this same model of building community through friendships might be done in a larger and perhaps even more intimate and respectful way with both genders. We might call it a laboratory of love. Let's discover how close we can get if there is great safety.

Indeed, let's imagine that we will transcend the "way it has always been done" even in the area of building community. If we study just which qualities have worked in forming and sustaining successful communities in specific situations, we get some clues as to what might work in new and different situations. For example, the phenomenon of eco-villages and co-housing has given us many examples of what worked, what bombed, and why.

Chapter 21   Needing Each Other

"There aren't enough iPods on earth to compensate for those missing friendships."

Bill McKibben

It was one of those rare moments when I felt both very vulnerable and very safe at the same time. I made eye contact with Jeff and said with clear intent, **"I need you."** It was simply a true statement from my heart that I was able to speak without shame. I gave voice to what we both knew was true. I know that when men say "Love ya man" to each other, parroting the beer commercial, they do actually mean it; they just don't feel safe enough to say it straight.

The very idea of needing others is a long lost concept in western—especially American—culture, which reveres the rugged individual, from archetypal cowboy frontiersman to the "I did it my way" entrepreneurial business hero. To need someone else is seen as weakness and a source of shame. So our authentic needs get covered over. In our MKP men's work we might see such a man as a "tiger in the office and pussycat at home." It's a playful metaphor for a male's allowing himself to be nurtured by his wife while always appearing publicly powerful.

Obviously this denial is going to be problem when we talk about needing each other and interdependence as an essential qualities of community. People who have not yet done enough personal awareness training may require some heart-opening experiences before feeling ready to experience truly needing other people, much less a whole community.

This book is intended for people strong and humble enough to risk feeling the open-hearted vulnerability that enables someone to look another in the eye and say "I need you." Think about doing that. Practice saying it to yourself in the mirror, to your partner, to your best friend. You'll get a feel for your readiness.

Imagine that you are a mountaineering team scaling Mt. Everest. You are tied together in your ascent and descent. The truth of "I need you" is totally apparent. How different is this from the daily reality of a planet rushing toward multiple and overlapping crises? It is simply the truth that we need each other.

Now that we acknowledge our mutual need and thus may be ready to live into it, let's look at some of the needs.

Marshall Rosenberg is someone I have admired for years as he has tenaciously brought his remarkable gift of "non-violent communication" into the world. Here is his list of our "needs" which I have annotated to show how they work within community.

Autonomy: choosing dreams, goals and values; making plans for their fulfillment, actualizing into the world.

Celebration: celebrating the creation of life and dreams fulfilled;
celebrating losses of our loved ones and hopes and dreams.

Integrity: authenticity; creativity; meaning and self-worth.

Interdependence: community; acceptance; appreciation; closeness; consideration; contribution; emotional safety; empathy; honesty; love; reassurance; respect; support; trust; and understanding.

Physical nurturance: air; food; movement; protection; rest; sexual expression; shelter; touch; water.

Play: fun and laughter, even in our work.

Spiritual communion: beauty; harmony; inspiration; order; peace; also their opposites, since community can be messy.

Now if this list of needs rightly names what we want, we might ask, "What sort of community would actually meet most of them?" And, "What might I give to receive the gift of having these needs met?" The answer to the first question might just be gift community. The second question suggests that as we come to know ourselves as the gift the answer is obvious. How are you the gift?

Chapter 22   Protecting Each Other

"... stories of Earth Community nurture a culture of partnership. They affirm the positive potentials of our human nature and show that realizing true prosperity, security, and meaning depends on creating vibrant, caring, interlinked communities that support all persons in realizing their full humanity."
David Korten

My website "Sacred Lifeboats" was launched in 2005. I warned of the coming crises. Now, six years later, mainstream opinion has accepted the reality of "peak oil," suggesting that the energy situation, at least, has become desperate enough that a stance of denial is no longer tenable. We must address the probability of a shredded safety net in challenging economic times. We need to take care of each other. We need to learn how to work together.

In the mid 1800s the world was changing from agrarian into industrial civilization and men were being fatally wounded in the factories and mines. Because there was no one to care for their families, men formed fraternal organizations like the Moose, Elks, Odd Fellows, Knights of Pythias, and so many others for mutual support. These mutual care systems allowed men to work together to protect their families and their community.

Now, as industrial civilization, as we have known it, winds down, work as we have known it is disappearing and we again find ourselves without adequate safety nets. It has become our task, as it was for our ancestors a century ago, to build the new mutual care systems for our transitional times. To do this we need trust, and that means bonded core communities. If and when we create such community, so many possibilities open up.

The following are some of the areas in which we can develop both simple and complex safety nets to take care of each other. And because many of our current systems need to be replaced, we will be building the future as we go.

Shared resources: Cars, trucks, tools, and equipment as well as a grand variety of community businesses such as small manufacturing, livestock, and greenhouse vegetable growing.

Finance: Shared purchase of food, transportation, and even shelter. With care of our money and new ways of exchange, we can rebuild communities as functioning economic entities. The collective decision-making needed to do so most likely will evolve organically out of deep trusting core communities.

Medical care: Private health insurance, shared information (e.g., about auto-immune and other mysterious diseases), private medical doctors and nursing on call in ways similar to what used to be called "the country doctor."

Health and Nutrition: Support each other in the knowledge and implementation of healthy practices. Reclaiming healthy foods known for centuries and lost in self serving corporate restrictions like raw milk. Nutritional counseling may become a priority for full self-care living. This makes the "country doctor" needed only in emergency situations.

Parenting: Make sure young mothers don't have to go to work and so can be present to raise their children during their earliest years.

Education: Transformative teaching to engage children's unique gifts and learning styles. Home schooling is already a model of how people are taking responsibility for the education of their children.

Safety: Share information about healthy food, water, medicines, etc. as well as the dangers of substances like transfats, Aspartame, MSG, and GMO foods.

Co-housing: As core community trust builds, possibilities of long-term housing arrangements might get very creative. The oversized "McMansions" may become available providing delightful shelter for people committed to each other and bonded as families.

Imagine your own "lifeboat." We can support each other in living sustainably and creatively. We can do this, but it requires the extensive trust and friendship available in bonded community. Together as we embrace the work in the world that genuinely serves us all, we will be in a position to design the new systems.

PART 4

OUR STORY
OF
LOST COMMUNITY

*We can never get enough
of what we don't really need.*

...contemporary folk wisdom

Chapter 23 Stranded Among Strangers

I cannot see how a country, a society, or a civilization can live while its communities die.   - Wendell Berry

In this part we will explore the questions of "Why has close community as we knew it gone away?" and "Why do we appear not to need each other?" These are big questions many of us seem either to ask or feel deep in our bones. In my own longing for community I sometimes quietly wondered, "Is it me, or is community just impossible?" Eventually as I asked enough questions I realized that the lack of close community in my country, race and my social class is a complex story.

My intention in this section is to invite us to view this dilemma of absent community from both the deeply personal and socio-economic perspectives. If we know why our society is the way it is, we may feel more competent to do what it takes to make wiser decisions about building the community we long for.

Starting with a very large context we see that humankind has never been here before. We are looking into the unknown. We have evolved from 150,000 generations of hunter-gatherer tribes to 50,000 generations of subsistence farmers. Now, in just a dozen generations, we have been industrial workers and used up billions of barrels of petroleum and tons of coal. The power of what seemed to be virtually free and unlimited energy created a life crazily different from anything our ancestor could ever have imagined.

Most poignantly we lost our connection with the earth, the mother that nurtures us all. We lost gratitude and our simple humble soft animal essence. Not too many generations ago we did not even know we had "selves" separate from our tribe. Suddenly we do not need anyone in particular, as other people have become interchangeable units serving us as we ignore our alienation from "our mother."

With a great deal of help from Charles Eisenstein, let us track this question of why community has been so dramatically diminished by following two seemingly sinple threads: money and food.

Chapter 24 Money: "Alone in a Crowd"

In The Ascent of Humanity (Panenthea Press, 2007), Charles Eisenstein presents an excellent and clear overview of just why and how community has become more difficulty in our current culture. In Section 2 of Chapter 4 he shows that with our money system our culture has devolved to a point at which, in specific and important ways, we really don't need each other. This entire chapter is an excerpt, with his permission. You might want to read this section a few times to understand the "truth that you already know" yet could not put in words. Understanding this truth will help a lot as we move into exploring what to do.

It should not be surprising that money is deeply implicated in the dissolution of community, because anonymity and competition are intrinsic to money as we know it. The anonymity of money is a function of its abstraction. The history of money is the history of the gradual abstraction of value from physical objects. Early forms of money possessed intrinsic value, and were distinguished from other objects of intrinsic value by their portability, storability, and universality. Whether camels, bags of grain, or jugs of oil, early media of exchange had an inherent value to nearly every member of the society.

As society specialized and trade flourished, more abstract forms of money developed that depended not on inherent value but on collective belief in their value. Why trade actual bags of grain when you can just trade representations of those bags? Paper money, and to a great extent coinage, depends for its value on collective perceptions rather than practical utility. You can't eat gold.

The next stage of the abstraction of value came with the divorce of money from even the representation of physical objects. With the abandonment of the gold standard in the 20th century, a dollar came to be worth. . . a dollar. Currency has become a completely abstract representation of value; indeed, the abstraction is so complete that it no longer really represents anything at all. The parallel with language is uncanny. Just as words have lost their mooring in the reality of our senses, "forcing us into increasingly exaggerated elocutions to communicate at all," so also has money become not just a representation of value but value itself. The last thirty years have witnessed the final step of this abstraction: the gradual elimination of physical currency altogether in favor of numbers in a computer.

Just as words increasingly mean nothing at all, money is also nearing a crisis in which, so disconnected from the utilitarian objects it once represented, it becomes nothing more than hunks of metal, pieces of paper, and bits in a computer. Our efforts to stave off this eventuality (of hyperinflation and currency collapse) mirror the logic of the technological fix, postponing the day of reckoning.

Money is abstract not only with regard to objects of utility, but also with regard to people. Anybody's money is the same. While camels or jugs of oil or any tangible object has an individuality connected with its origin, money is completely generic and thus completely anonymous. Nothing in the digits of your savings account statement tells you who that money came from. One person's money is as good as another's. It is no accident that our society, based increasingly on money, is also increasingly a generic and anonymous society. Money is how the society of the Machine enacts the standardization and depersonalization implicit in its mass scale and division of labor. But more than just a means to implement depersonalization, money also pushes it further.

To see how, let us return to the paradise of financial independence, ignoring for now that the security it promises is but a temporary illusion, and instead look at the results when it is actually achieved. Often, it is when the semblance of independence is achieved that its emptiness becomes most apparent. Simply observe that the financially independent individual, among other equally independent individuals, has no basis for community except for the effort to "be nice" and "make friends". Underneath even the most well-motivated social gathering is the knowledge: We don't really need each other. Contemporary parties, for example, are almost always based on consumption—of food, drink, drugs, sports, or other forms of entertainment. We recognize them as frivolous. This sort of fun really doesn't matter, and neither do the friendships based on fun. Does anybody ever become close by partying together?

Actually, I don't think that joint consumption is even fun. It only passes the time painlessly by covering up a lack, and leaves us feeling all the more empty. The significance of the superficiality of our social leisure becomes apparent when we contrast that sort of "fun" with a very different activity, play. Unlike joint consumption, play is by nature creative. Joint creativity fosters relationships that are anything but superficial. But when our fun, our entertainment, is itself the object of purchase, and is created by distant and anonymous specialists for our consumption (movies, sports contests, music), then we become consumers and not producers of fun. We are no longer players.

Play is the production of fun; entertainment is the consumption of fun. When the neighbors watch the Superbowl together they are consumers; when they organize a game of touch football (alas, the parks are empty these days) they are producers. When they watch music videos together they consume; when they play in a band they produce. Only through the latter activity is there the possibility of getting to know each other's strengths and limitations, character and inner resources. In contrast, the typical cocktail party, dinner party, or Superbowl party affords little opportunity to share much of oneself, because there is nothing to do. (And have you noticed how any attempt to share oneself in such settings seems contrived, uncomfortable, awkward, inappropriate, or embarrassing?) Besides, real intimacy comes not from telling about yourself—your childhood, your relationships, your health problems, etc.—but from joint creativity, which brings out your true qualities, invites you to show that aspect of yourself needed for the task at hand. Later, when intimacy has developed, telling about oneself may come naturally—or it may not even be necessary.

Have you ever wondered why your childhood friendships were closer, more intimate, more bonded than those of adulthood? At least that's how I remember mine. It wasn't because we had heart-to-heart conversations about our feelings. With our childhood friends we felt a closeness that probably wasn't communicated in words. We did things together and created things together. From an adult's perspective our creativity was nothing but games: our play forts and cardboard box houses and pretend tea parties and imaginary sports teams and teddy bear families were not real. As children, though, these activities were very real to us indeed; we were absolutely in earnest and invested no less a degree of emotion in our make-believe than adults do in theirs.

Yes, the adult world is make-believe too. Roles and costumes, games and pretenses contribute to a vast story. When we become aware of it, we sense the artificiality of it all and feel, perhaps, like a child playing grown-up. The entire edifice of culture and technology is built on stories, composed of symbols, about how the world is. Usually we don't notice; we think it is all "for real". Our stories are mostly unconscious. But the new edifice that will rise from the ruins of the old will be built on very different stories of self and world, and these stories will be consciously told. We will go back to play.

As children the things we did together mattered to us. To us they were real; we cared about them intensely and they evoked our full being. In contrast, most of the things we do together as adults for the sake of fun and friendship do not matter. We recognize them as frivolous, unnecessary, and relegate them to our "spare time." A child does not relegate play to spare time, unless forced to.

I remember the long afternoons of childhood when my friends and I would get totally involved in some project or other, which became for that time the most important thing in the universe. We were completely immersed, in our project and in our group. Our union was greater than our mere sum as individuals; the whole was greater than the sum of the parts. The friendships that satisfy our need for connection are those that make each person more than themselves. That extra dimension belongs to both partners and to neither, akin to the "fifth voice" that emerges in a barbershop quartet out of the harmonics of the four. In many of my adult relationships I feel diminished, not enlarged. I don't feel like I've let go of boundaries to become part of something greater than my self; instead I find myself tightly guarding my boundaries and doling out only that little bit of myself that is safe or likeable or proper. Others do the same. We are reserved. We are restrained.

Our reservedness should not be too surprising, because there is little in our adult friendships that compels us to be together. We can get together and talk, we can get together and eat and talk, we can get together and drink and talk. We can watch a movie or a concert together and be entertained. There are many opportunities for joint consumption but few for joint creativity, or for doing things together about which we care intensely. At most we might go sailing or play sports with friends, and at least we are working together toward a common purpose, but even so we recognize it as a game, a pastime. The reason adult friendships seem so superficial is that they are superficial. The reason we can find little to do besides getting together and talking, or getting together to be entertained, is that our society's specialization has left us with little else to do. Thus the teenager's constant refrain: "There's nothing to do." He is right. As we move into adulthood, in place of play we are offered consumption, in place of joint creativity, competition, and in place of playmates, the professional colleague.

The feeling "We don't really need each other" is by no means limited to leisure gatherings. What better description could there be of the loss of community in today's world? We don't really need each other. We don't need to know the person who grows, ships, and processes our food, makes our clothing, builds our house, creates our music, makes or fixes our car; we don't even need to know the person who takes care of our babies while we are at work. We are dependent on the role, but only incidentally on the person fulfilling that role. Whatever it is, we can just pay someone to do it (or pay someone else to do it) as long as we have money. And how do we get money? By performing some other specialized role that, more likely than not, amounts to other people paying us to do something for them. This is what I call the monetized life, in which nearly all aspects of existence have been either converted to commodities or assigned a financial value.

The necessities of life have been given over to specialists, leaving us with nothing meaningful to do (outside our own area of expertise) but to entertain ourselves. Meanwhile, whatever functions of daily living that remain to us are mostly solitary functions: driving places, buying things, paying bills, cooking convenience foods, doing housework. None of these demand the help of neighbors, relatives, or friends. We wish we were closer to our neighbors; we think of ourselves as friendly people who would gladly help them. But there is little to help them with. In our house-boxes, we are self-sufficient. Or rather, we are self-sufficient in relation to the people we know but dependent as never before on total strangers living thousands of miles away.

Times of crisis still can bring us closer to our neighbors. When a health crisis renders us unable to perform the simple functions of daily survival, or a natural disaster or social crisis ruptures the supplies of food, electricity, and transportation that make us dependent on remote strangers but independent of our neighbors, we are glad to help each other out. Reciprocal relationships quickly form. But usually, we don't help out our neighbors very much because there is nothing to help them with.

For the typical suburbanite, what is there to do with friends? We can cook together for fun, but we don't need each other's help in producing food. We don't need each other to create shelter or clothing. We don't need each other to care for us when we are sick. All these functions have been given over to paid specialists who are generally strangers. In an age of mass consumption, we don't need each other to produce entertainment. In an age of paid childcare, we hesitate to ask each other for help with the children. In the age of TV and the Internet, we don't need each other to tell us the news. In fact, not only is there little to do together, there is equally little to talk about. All that is left is the weather, the lawn, celebrities and sports. "Serious" topics are taboo. We can fill up our social gatherings with words, it is true, but we are left feeling empty, sending those words into an aching void that words can never fill.

And so we find in our culture a loneliness and hunger for authenticity that may well be unsurpassed in history. We try to "build community," not realizing that mere intention is not enough when separation is built into the very social and physical infrastructure of our society. To the extent that this infrastructure is intact in our lives, we will never experience community. Community is incompatible with the modern lifestyle of highly specialized work and complete dependence on other specialists outside that work. It is a mistake to think that we live ultraspecialized lives and somehow add another ingredient called "community" on top of it all. Again, what is there really to share? Not much that matters, to the extent that we are independent of neighbors and dependent on faceless institutions and distant strangers. We can try: go meet the neighbors, organize a potluck, a listserve, a party. Such community can never be real, because the groundwork of life is already anonymity and convenience.

When we pay professionals to grow our food, prepare our food, create our entertainment, make our clothes, build our houses, clean our houses, treat our illnesses, and educate our children, what's left? What's left on which to base a community? Real communities are interdependent.

Now we have reached the sinister core of financial independence: it tends to isolate us in a world of strangers. It is strangers whom we pay to perform the functions listed above. It doesn't really matter who grows your food—if they have a problem, you can always pay someone else to do it. This phrase encapsulates much about our modern society. When all functions are standardized and narrowly defined, it does not matter too much who fills them. We can always pay someone else to do it. As an individual, it is hard not to feel dispensable, a cog in the machine. We feel dispensable because, in terms of survival, in terms of all the economic functions of life, we are dispensable.

If you buy food from the supermarket deli, the people behind the kitchen doors, whom you never meet, are dispensable. If they quit, even if they die, someone else can be hired to fill their role. The same goes for the laborers in Indonesia who make the clothes you buy at the superstore. The same goes for the engineers who design your computer. We rely on their roles, their functions, but as individual humans they are expendable. Maybe you are a nice, friendly person who actually exchanges friendly greetings with the cashier who's worked for five years at the local supermarket, but while you may be dependent on her role, the specific person filling this role is unimportant. It does not really matter if you get along with this person, or even know her name. She could be fired or die and it would make little difference in your life. It would not be much of a loss. Unless you live in a very small town, you probably will never know what happened to her or ever think to ask. All the more so for the vast majority of the people who sustain our material lives. They, unlike cashiers, are utterly faceless to us.

Because the economy depends on our roles, but does not care which individuals fill these roles, we suffer an omnipresent anxiety and insecurity borne of the fact that the world can get along just fine without us. We are easily replaced. Of course, for our friends and loved ones—people who know us personally—we are irreplaceable. But with the increasingly fine division of labor and mass scale of modern society, these are fewer and fewer, as more and more social functions enter the monetized realm. Thus we live in fear, anxiety, and insecurity, and justifiably so, because we are easily replaceable in the roles we perform to earn money.

We can get along fine without you. We'll just pay someone else to do it.

Chapter 25   Food: Needing Connection

"Either we are in the universe to inhabit the lovely eternity of our souls and grow real, or else we might as well dedicate our days to shopping and kill time watching talk shows."

John O'Donohue

In Greek mythology, those who insult the goddess of earthly plenty are usually punished with hungers that can't be satisfied. We see chronic over-consumption all around us as too many people move too fast, trying desperately to get enough of what they don't really need. Because we can see it "out there," we may also see it inside ourselves and so perhaps we can heal this unholy hunger.

Tellingly, we actually define ourselves as a "consumer" culture. Programming for consumption runs deep in nearly all of us. The corporations haven't spent billions on advertising for nothing. But just what are we really so hungry for?

Because food is a pervasive item of consumption, we might look there for a clue. In a provocative essay on food called "Reuniting the Self: Autoimmunity, Obesity, and the Ecology of Health," Charles Eisenstein touches on something causally profound:

> "All the individual is aware of is a hunger, a need for something more. The fact that obese people often eat when they are not physically hungry offers a clue to what is going on. Indeed, they are hungry—they just aren't hungry for food. They are hungry for connection.

> "Food is the most tangible, direct confirmation of our connection to a living universe that loves us. On a primal biological level, the act of eating tells us, "I exist" and "I am loved." Indeed, food is the most basic expression of love, a token of intimacy, of bringing an outsider into the realm of self. That is why it is customary in most countries to offer food to a guest, and why it is rude to refuse it. To feed another is, in this sense, an intimate act, an opening of the sacred boundaries of self."

> "When, as today, this intimate act has become a subject of commerce, and food a commodity, the entire food system reeks of obscenity."

"Obesity is usually taken as a symptom of excess, but in fact the reverse is true. Obesity, and the other enlargements I have mentioned, are actually symptoms of the most profound destitution ever to visit the human race. The bloated lifestyles of the American rich harbor an inner poverty exactly equal to the Third World poverty that enables those lifestyles. **Half the world cannot get enough to eat, and the other half cannot get enough no matter how much they eat.** It is a complete tapestry, perfect and horrifying."

"Consigned by modern civilization to a tiny, isolated self, we suffer from a powerful unmet need for love and connection."

Community may be the end of hunger. Consider that with the support of our core communities we just might heal this chronic social hunger. To start, ask yourself how often you eat alone, with family or friend, and especially with a community. Do you share a communal meal at least once a week, month or year?

In our model of core gift community we suggest once a week. What would it take for you to share a meal every week? Here is a starting point for ending the hunger that our culture instills in us but cannot satisfy. It may be challenging to arrange for the weekly communal meal, but it is doable because the longing for it is already in your heart.

Chapter 26   Beyond Addiction: Face in the Gutter

One of the harshest comparisons I have heard about our lack of community is the metaphor of alcohol addiction. What will it take for us to know that we need each other? How can we break from our "non-negotiable" way of live?

Addicts will say anything, promise anything, but in the pervasive lie of their addiction no change is effective until they're face down in the gutter. Then and only then, they may get treatment or join Alcohols Anonymous. Only then will they surrender into being powerless and accept the support of a community at daily or weekly meetings where they may, one day at a time, stay sober.

Our addiction to our "way of life" is analogous. We seem to rationalize every act of consumption—from one more cookie to invading Iraq to assure our access to oil. I sometimes look in the mirror and suggest to the guy I see there, "If you rode your bike 10 blocks to a meeting, maybe just once a week, it might even be healthy for you."

We have become progressively addicted to our "consumer life" over the last century. Despite the twisted sense that it is "non-negotiable," our levels of consumption and their associated pollution are simply unsustainable. And as with a chemical addiction, we feel the pain of withdrawal as we are forced to change. Millions of us have already lost savings, good jobs, or homes or know others who are in this situation. Will this motivate us to reach out for authentic community?

I see good news in that many of our children and grandchildren were raised with a certain empathy and conscious knowing of Gaia that my generation did not have. They are not addicted. For example, many have chosen to be vegetarians or vegans or to eat only raw food. I have been greatly impressed with their wisdom and courage to do the right thing. Yet my addiction is such that I still have changed only some of my eating habits, such as only occasional red meat. I so honor these younger generations who are so much more free inside than we ever were.

Perhaps more of us can beat our addiction to consumer culture and the imperial politics it entails. A community of people with whom we can share the transition is enormously helpful as we can actively support each other in making the needed changes. And with the work of transition comes a sense of collaborating, bonding and strengthening that community feeling we have been longing for.

Chapter 27 Beyond Cynicism: Do What We Can Do

Perhaps the chapters in this part of the book have induced the feeling of being overwhelmed and helpless. So what do we do and how did it get that way? If everyone we know wants friends, community and family, why do we live in a super-wealthy culture of consumption yet feel scarcity, isolation and fear? Seems like a fair question. And the answers are complex. The search requires us to follow the logic of two direct questions: **Who does it serve to be the way it is?** and **Who has the power to make it that way or change it?**

Assuming I had the answers to these questions I went into resignation and cynicism. I felt stuck, grumbling about the "powers-that-be." Eventually my cynical-self was inspired by some relentless optimists. They knew just as much as I did about how bad it is, but they kept looking for that pony in the horse-pucky pile. For ten years my friend Jeff Golden was a great local radio talk show host who interviewed guests from coast to coast. Every day at the very end of his show he would say five words which were the theme of his show: **"Do what you can do!"** The saying reflected Jeff's knowing that we each have our gift and that small efforts add up.

At first I saw this stance as naive' optimism – after all what can one person do? And with all my clever insights I would go back to cynicism and resignation. I would make remarks in political conversations like, "You don't really want to hear my opinion of the president; it will bum you out."

One day I read in Peter Block's book *Community: The Structure of Belonging*
 "Resignation is the ultimate act of powerlessness and a stance against
 possibility. It is a passive form of control. It is born of our cynicism and
 loss of faith. What <u>we</u> are resigning from is the future and what we are
 embracing is the past. None of us is strong enough to carry the dead weight
 of others' resignation or even our own. Resignation ultimately alienates us
 and destroys community. It is the spiritual cause of isolation and not
 belonging. Be aware of resignation, for it presents itself as if data and
 experience were on its side."

I said, "Well, look at that. I know so much about the world situation and I'm using it to stay stuck." In moments of insight like this there is only one thing to do—take a deep breath and **do what you can do.** I've been working on this book every day since that moment.

So, here's what we can do. Let's get aligned in supporting each other in "doing what we can do." Together, as community, we can weather the storms of whatever may come and have a good time bonding as we work together and support each other. Feel being blessed and blessing the projects and tasks and gifts that each of us bring forward. As your tribe gathers, feel all that creative joyous energy in the same room at the same time.

A fable from: Beyond Civilization: Humanity's Next Great Adventure
By: Daniel Quinn

Once upon a time life evolved on a certain planet, bringing for the many different social organizations--packs, pods, flocks, herds, and so on. One species whose members were unusually intelligent developed a unique social organization called a tribe: Tribalism worked well for them for millions of years, but there came a time when they decided to experiment with a new social organization (called civilization) that was hierarchal rather than tribal.

Before long, those at the top of the hierarchy were living in great luxury, enjoying perfect leisure and having the best of everything. A larger class of people below them lived very well and had nothing to complain about. But the masses living at the bottom of the hierarchy didn't like it at all. They worked and lived like pack animals, struggling just to stay alive.

"This isn't working," the masses said. "The tribal way was better. We should return to that way." But the ruler of the hierarchy told them, "We've put that primitive life behind us forever. We can't go back to it."
"If we can't go back," the masses said, "then let's go forward--on to something different."
"That can't be done," the ruler said, "because nothing different is possible. Nothing can be *beyond* civilization. Civilization is a final, unsurpassable invention."
"But no invention is ever unsurpassable. The steam engine was surpassed by the gas engine. The radio was surpassed by television. The calculator was surpassed by the computer. Why should civilization be different."
"I don't know *why* it's different," the ruler said. "It just *is.*"

But the masses didn't believe this--and neither do I.

The tribe, in fact, is just a wonderfully efficient social organization that renders making a living easy for all--unlike civilization, which renders it easy for a privileged few and hard for the rest.

Beyond civilization isn't a geographical space up in the mountains or on some remote desert isle. It is a cultural space that opens up among people with new minds. Old minds think: *How do we solve these problems"?*
New minds think: ***How do we make happen what we want to happen?"***

SECTION TWO: HOW-TO

Rusty calls for committed community, now!

PART 5

GETTING STARTED

*"No more prizes for forecasting the rain...
Only prizes for building the Ark."*
Don Beck

Chapter 28   Introduction

I've been deeply committed to human transformation for 37 years. I have studied the maturation process and been instrumental in creating trainings to facilitate people's opening into greater complexity. I believe we can consciously include our competent, autonomous individual selves as we transcend into interdependent community people. We are ready, let's go.

Given the rapid social changes and the state of our world, we don't have time to allow community to form the way it used to. This second section of the book is designed to guide you—actually walk you step by step—through thinking about the creating community you want. The discussion draws on decades of learning from people's experiences in co-housing and eco-villages to provide direction about how to find the people you want, how to invite them, get to know them, evaluate their readiness, make an informed mutual decision, and finally initiate them into core community.

Commit Yourself.   When we choose to take action for the safety of our selves, family, community or planet, we become part of the evolving new culture. We do what is in front of us to do, and then discover we are changing the world. We find that small actions have profound effects and that indeed we have "become the change."

The greatest single thing we can do as individuals to create a more beautiful world is **decide that it is worth doing**. So, the very act of co-creating your authentic community is a world-changing thing to do.

When you make that first phone call to invite those two friends over for a pot-luck supper and a conversation about imagining a core gift community, you begin a process that will reverberate towards our grandchildren and beyond. That small act opens the possibility of building mutual food security, economic safety-nets, environmental stewardship, and other social inventions. These inventions in turn can become templates for replication by neighborhoods, cities, and other larger social groupings. Indeed, our process of creating what we personally need is also a way of co-creating a future pathway for humanity.

Chapter 29   Champions with Vision

Don't ask what the world needs.
Ask what makes you come alive, and go do it.
Because what the world needs is people who have come alive.

Howard Thurman

Over the decades I've embraced an axiom for the one thing that works to get things done: **"Nothing happens without a champion!"**

Each gift community begins with a founder who feels called to champion or catalyze a vision of a core community. This champion offers the gift of getting the community started. I believe such champions are essential to the success of a community. Without these self-starters with people skills, nothing much will happen. These are the ones that Malcolm Gladwell in his popular book *The Tipping Point* calls "connectors" because they have a gift for social connections.

These champions of community must hold the vision as well as motivate its manifestation. In a business context they would be called project managers. And as they say, "No project manager, no project."

In my experience everyone talks about community but very few do anything about it. Right now you may be feeling personally called to be a champion, or you might be thinking about who you know, that has the requisite character and skills.

A "Champion" might begin with one person who invites one or two others who share the vision. We'll assume "Champion" as plural from this point on.

The ideal champion serves as a labor of love, launching her community as she envisions it, trusting the wisdom of the emerging group, and lets it go as soon as it can thrive on its own. Champions know they don't need permission from people to lead them. People are waiting for them to point the way and show how to reach the destination. Champions step out because it is important to them and people need their leadership. And they step out of the way when the job is done.

Qualifications of champions to be core community visionaries

1. Desire to have a personal community of their own.
2. Are usually "self starters" with entrepreneurial qualities.
3. Can make a commitment, and inspire others to do the same.
4. Have a deep belief in the desired results and a willingness to persevere.
5. Have done enough "inner work" to know how essential psycho-spiritual maturity is and how to gauge it in others. This is requisite for the on-going "onion peeling" of self-witnessing transparency that characterizes authentic community.
6. Trained, or willing to be trained, in the skills of organizing, screening people, shadow work, holding safe space, doing ceremonies and initiation.
7. Capable of maintaining balance through feedback and response. They can listen for what works and discard what does not.
8. Know how to "work them selves out of a job" and when to get out of the way once their start-up skills are no longer needed.

Responsibilities of the champions/founders

1. Determining the vision and core values: Who we are. The champion must find the vision in their heart and hold it with conviction until… others carry it with them. Their vision and values may reflect the model and suggestions of this book or whatever inspiration calls them.

2. Determining the structure: How we do things. Someone must decide just what will be the arrangements, organization and composition of the new community? This may include membership guidelines, group size, time together, governance, finances, and conflict resolution.

3. Developing membership criteria: Identify the people right for our community? What age, background and psycho-spiritual maturity are we seeking? Determine the level of commitment for membership, duration of provisional membership, the form and intention of the initiation.

4. Holding the center: Stay on task until the group has embraced the founding vision and values. *It is important to not "give it-away" too soon or hold it too long!* And when the community has become self-perpetuating with the next wave of leadership bringing their gifts forward, then, the champions relax and let go. They then become "elders" with a "tribal memory" of the vision, values, and story of our community.

The Vision of Champions

"Committees do not create vision, people create vision."

Peter Senge

Vision is the glue of community: The vision is a possibility and the fundamental reason for our existence. Our vision is what truly matters, as it is something more important and larger than the members. It's what our community is here to do together.

Vision Statement: Here we define our purpose rooted in our values. Whether you call it vision or purpose, the statement represents the essential reason for the community's existence. The people we want are those who share a vision to make the world a better place. Peter Senge describes vision statements as "an image of our desired future, a picture of the future we seek to create." In writing a vision statement, it's best to use the present tense, as if it were happening now.

Examples of community "vision statements": We exist to change the world one community at a time. We band together for survival, sustainability, and co-creation of new culture. We create a safe world for our great grandchildren. We model a more ecologically sound and socially/culturally sustainable urban way of life.

Core Values: Our values are traits or qualities that advise our vision. Our values determine our decisions and guide our lives. A healthy community needs shared values about how life works and how humans relate. Each member recognizes and shares certain "truths" and chooses certain behaviors aligned with her values. Please see chapter 31 for some possible community values.

Goals: Community goals represent what people commit themselves to do, often within a few months. Goals are always measurable: exactly how we will do it, by when, by who, how big, how much and what kind? Specific, realizable goals are the milestones we expect to reach by a specific time.

Chapter 30   Zoe - Actual Steps

Thought is a blossom; language the bud; action the fruit.
                                    Ralph Waldo Emerson

How to Go from Thought to Action: Core Community

The second part of this book focuses on Core Community, the specifics of how to develop a personal family of choice with commitments to values, place and shared years together. For many this level of commitment may initially appear too daunting. If this is the case you might want to consider hosting a Gift Circle. A Gift Circle is an excellent vehicle for friendships to deepen as it directly demonstrates that we do need each other. It can be a "way in" as it is far more casual with virtually no commitments. A Gift Circle (see Chapter 10. P. 35) is a natural step towards deepening relationships and is potentially useful for building your Core Community with those who want to co-create more lasting community.

When we began this work we had no template to follow. We wanted to move beyond the thicket of endless talk about building community to taking action. We knew we had to find the middle ground between slowly getting to know people and igniting the fire of intentional focus needed to catalyze a committed group. We organized circles, played interactive theater games, shared our ideas, conversations and endless potlucks. We had not yet encountered the idea of Gift Culture or Gift Circles but we were clear about the need for a core, committed community.

This went on for years as we wrestled with how to champion a community and choose a core group. Eventually we gathered the courage and began inviting friends to step into this vision of "fictive kinship". At least a dozen said "no" or" My town is enough community!" or "We've got another project right now." However, truly perseverance furthered and eventually, with the genuine interest of a few, we gathered a momentum of necessity that brought us to the next step.

Gateway One: Written Testament of Intention

So, how did we actually proceed from the invitation to the building of our core gift community? Oddly enough, the first step was creating an application form. This enabled people to share the truth of their histories and the truth of their longings, as well as references of people who could vouch for them. Writing a brief account of your intention, where you have been, and where you want to go, then sealing it with your signature is the first gateway. Though it might seem like normal paperwork, it is a ritual in which hand, heart, and mind together create a testament of intention. It was an important threshold to cross.

The day Bill asked me to fill out my paperwork was cold. Even so, I wrapped up in a coat and shut the sliding glass door after me as I stepped onto the porch. I wanted to be by myself as I composed my testament. Different voices in my head held quite a conference during the process. The dissident rebel, the cautionary advisor, the resentful feminist; they all spoke with vigor. I witnessed them as I wrote the easy parts and then the difficult parts of my past and stated my intention and reasons for a deep family of choice.

After I dated and signed it, I went back inside and handed it to Bill. "Now, it is your turn to make your application." And he did. That simple act of each of us formally going on record marked a turning point from "thought to action". Now we could invite the others who had expressed sincere interest to pass through this gateway.

This step moved Bill and I from being founders to also being provisional members of our budding core gift community. Others now began to step into Provisional Membership. Our attention became keenly focused on the people who had taken this next step. Already a new level of commitment had emerged. We began to look for ways to show up for each other's needs.

Bill and I also began to embrace their families in a new way as well. Personally I am not fond of football, but on several Friday nights cheering on a teenage football player was the place I chose to be. When an aging parent or a child landed in the hospital or emergency room, we took the time to go and sit with our friends, offering them our support. When two of our provisional members were unavailable to be with their father in a nursing home, Bill and I filled in. This extension of old fashioned caring built a framework of trust for the community. We modeled what we wanted to deepen into.

Gateway Two: The Ritual of Spoken Declaration

One day we were helping to pack up, clean, and paint the home of a couple in the group. When we broke for lunch the next ritual gateway spontaneously manifested. Bill and I had been discussing the importance of gathering people to our core community who are fundamentally fulfilled to overflowing in their core and want to give their gifts. As a way of anchoring this, we proposed that we speak of what we have to give each other.

The Ponderosa pines and Douglas firs in southern Oregon are often fragrant when the resin on their bark warms in the sun. Occasionally eagles glide through the sky above these aromatic tree crowns of needles. That day was such a day. As we shared our sincere and deep "I give yous", a golden eagle swooped quite majestically above our heads. Each person spoke of the gifts that were natural to their essence in a profoundly pure way.

"I give you my tenacity, my relentless focus, my tools, my ability to build things with my hands, my creativity, my playfulness, my devotion to transparency and openness . . . ."

As we proceeded around the table our words and transparency dropped us deeper and deeper into a timeless space; Just the warm wind in the pines and the eagle disappearing into sky. Then we were complete; so connected and open hearted. We blessed the moment, noticed its unique quality, and went back to the work of cleaning and packing up their hand-built home of fourteen years.

While approaching our next level of commitment into full membership, there were times when I found myself in distress. I had begun to ask myself how was I possibly going to be able to hold even more dear friends in my life, especially when Bill talked about 30 to 150 people in a core gift community. I felt worn out with just five. But occasions such as that ritual moment when we declared our gifts to each other have offered such balm to the soul. The subtle food that comes from this new level of relating is difficult to discuss in words. What I have come to discover is that as more people step into the core community, more of the tasks of caring and support are shared.

Gateway Three: Membership

Many months passed of provisional membership before we set time aside for our formal evening of initiation into full membership. This gateway marked not only the passage into full membership but also the moment when we all now equally shared decision-making powers.

In preparation for the initiation, I looked for symbolic objects that were simple and yet natural to our home environment. I wanted a way for us to literally hold in our hands our core values so I created eight discs out of heavy duty watercolor paper. Each painting I cut out in circles about the size of a CD so they could easily be held. I painted them and edged them in gold paint, then added the words of a core value on each of eight discs. These have turned out to be important and delightful tools for our membership process. Earlier, one of the group had brought us a candelabra made by a women's collective in Mexico and another had gifted us with a large red candle with the word Love inscribed on it. These came to be our ritual fire. A smooth river rock for each person was placed on an earthen plate. There was also a bowl that we filled with water gathered from The Chalice Well in England and mixed with water from a nearby spring outside of our town. These items were placed on a table in our freshly cleaned meeting room along with a vase of fresh flowers.

We greeted each person at the door as they arrived. I received their potluck offering for our dinner feast and brought the platters to the kitchen while Bill waved white sage smoke around each person as a ceremonial gesture of cleansing. They then in silence removed their shoes and entered the space set for our meeting, a space beyond ordinary time. When all were gathered, I sang a welcoming song. Bill and I spoke the intent of the evening to welcome them into full membership, perhaps for the rest of our lives, but at the very minimum for our agreed time of three years. Then we sat in a circle and passed around the Core Value painted discs one by one. We spoke carefully about how we held each inscribed value as significant and what questions we still had. The tall candles burned down low.

We then washed each other's hands and faces with warm water and washcloths and tenderly dried them as a symbol of how we would take care of each other. Bill and I asked them to sit with eyes closed and think of something they were grateful for. Then we took turns placing our hands on their heads and silently blessing them each with our loving intention for their greatest good. As this concluded, we all stood up together and greeted each other with spoken gratitude for their gift to our life, gazing eye to eye, seeing each other and being seen. The deepening was exquisite. The celebratory feast that followed was just as sweet. The healthy, delicious food is another testament to the loving abundance that we share.

Members Initiate Founders

Since Bill and I, the founding champions of our core gift community, had not been initiated, the new members decided that this was their next obvious step. At the appointed hour we arrived at our friend's home where one of the men was awaiting us. Using spare words, he led us to the center of a stone labyrinth where another beautiful friend handed us blindfolds and solemnly instructed us to put them on and informed us that we would be guided to our next destination. In honor of this occasion we had dressed in our finest, and I was very glad we did as this guide was magnificently attired. First Bill was guided from the labyrinth. I waited in blindfolded stillness until I was encouraged to proceed, advised from behind of turns or obstacles in the path. My sensing was heightened as I felt the coolness of an arbor then the heat of the sun. We seemed to go on for a very long time. Eventually I heard the sounds of flowing water and I was halted. While still blindfolded, songs were sung to us and words of commitment and appreciation spoken. These sounds cascaded over my whole being as each person spoke. We then moved forward even further and our shoes and blindfolds were removed. There we were at the edge of a beautiful rushing stream. As we splashed and waded into the cold water my heart was as light and joyful as a songbird. We held each other with such warmth as we scrambled back up the hill for another delicious feast. We told stories and played until the sun was long set and the candles on the candelabra had turned to light.

Deep within us rests a vulnerable, pure and childlike essence. To rediscover this joy with friends has been of great delight. The design of our rituals may not be suited to your group so, I encourage you to find what does. These practices are not set in stone. It is in the moment of spontaneous invention where heart touching power is found. These kinds of co-creative actions along with other "practical" acts of service will bond your group as they have ours.

Core Gift Community groups recognize that they need each other. Too often gatherings such as Saturday night football and social parties are rife with the sentiment, "I don't need you" so that authentic connection rarely occurs and there is little place for the shinning of people's gifts. This is where both Gift Circles and Core Gift Communities bust loose the negative trance of lack (Old story: "What we most need is money, not each other.") and throw open the doors to positive entrancement. (New story:" We are deeply connected gifts to each other; generously and abundantly supported in the web of life.") With this true relationship to self and other and a willingness to be outrageously generous and receptive, you can take steps to create exquisite culture.

Chapter 31   Core Community Values

> *The single most important cultural trait is social rules benefiting the group as a whole.*   Derrick Jensen

A stable community needs shared values or principles about how life works and how humans best relate. Each member recognizes and shares certain "truths" and chooses certain behaviors. The following are some values the authors consider deeply important. You are welcome to borrow any or all of them for your community.

1.   **Living Sustainability:** We recognize the challenges of the times in which we live. Given our current economic, environmental, energy, social and cultural situation, **we choose** to design our community to be resilient. As obsolete structures come to their natural end, we develop new systems and build the needed safety nets to meet our common needs in a rapidly changing world.

2.   **Choosing Place:** We observe that part of the cultural alienation we suffer, is our high mobility. We are done moving and we're committed to live in this place. **We choose** to stay in place to actually be physically near the people whom we hold as our core community and develop relationship with the natural world around us. We live in our own separate homes, but close enough to our community to be merely bicycle distance away. Shared homes is always an option that becomes more likely as people bond and trust more deeply.

3.   **Commitment to Each Other:** We know that the people with whom we spend time and energy will become our closest friends and core community. **We choose** to bring a new level of attention to specific deeper friendships instead of many acquaintances. We carefully and purposefully select members with psycho-social-spiritual skills mature enough to be able to open their hearts to healthy relationships, touch the divine and co-create new culture. We commit to these seasoned friends as we share the joy of growing together over the decades.

4.   **Personal Integrity:** We define moral responsibility as personal integrity or truth. In this maturation men and women engender the trust, which becomes the glue of the community. Without this moral integrity we debilitate the community as a parasite or burden. Therefore **we choose** to live our lives in integrity and be accountable to each other as we commit to always tell the truth.

5. **Gender Respect:** We recognize patterns of abuse done to both genders and planet by the patriarchal dominating culture over too many centuries. Therefore **we choose** to live informed by mutual gender respectfulness. We practice clear boundaries and transparency to allow love and true harmony between women and men.

6. **Durable Community**: We acknowledge that we cannot do it alone. Therefore **we choose** the task of building deep loving long-term community. As part of our healing and evolving process we explore new ways of "being" with each other. We seek authentic intimacy as our joyous and creative path into this adventure of innovating community. We build stable, gender safe, committed, trusting communities to increase our mutual support and security.

7. **Culture co-Creation:** We recognize that the times call for conscious action toward sustainability. **We choose** to be part of the evolving culture as we take action for the safety of our selves, family, community and planet. We co-create our future trusting that within the safety of our core community the needed social, environmental, economic and other "safety-net" inventions will become functional. These may become templates for use in the larger world.

8. **Celebration of Relationship with Divine Presence:** We understand the sacred interdependent relationship of all things as the natural law, which we as humans live within. Therefore **we choose** to stay conscious of our spiritual place within and co-creational process in the order of the universe.

Note here on "Spirituality" as a significant value: Champions will want to consider some sort of acknowledgment of The Divine. Most of us need a way of establishing a relationship of respect with that Something Greater than ourselves. We found this to be a great challenge and eventually chose the words above, which is a long name for God, however it gives plenty of room for inclusion of many belief systems of a wider spectrum of people.

Chapter 32   Structure of Community

Structure is defined as arrangement, organization, configuration and composition. A community requires some shape and composition. The structure of a core community ideally will follow the vision and values of the people creating it. That is to say, the champions will need to get most of these in place fairly early in the communities' development. These become the intentions of "how we operate" that the members agree to abide by.

Below are some structural components. Many of these are referred to in detail in later sections to allow deeper understanding. This list of our suggestions is grounded in the values and commitments or agreements designed so that members will get what they want.

We Meet Face to Face: We value actually being together as opposed to "virtual" communities of long distance connections. Therefore we choose to live in close proximity, meet often and regularly. To make sure this happens we make commitments of "long-term" duration.

We Live Near Each Other: We want to actually be physically with the people in our core community, therefore we make a commitment to living in this place, this bio-region, this neighborhood. We commit to staying right here, caring for, stewarding this land. And though we mostly live in separate homes, they are all within "bicycle distance" of each other by conscious choice. This keeps us in proximity. (see Chapter 35)

We Make A Long Term Commitment: Because we intend to stay together we have committed to our "core community" for a minimum time span of 3 years. We consciously choose to pursue life long friendships with each other and with our families. We know our community will be there to care for us, our families and perhaps even bury each other when the time comes.

We Spend Spacious, Regular Time Together: We recognize how consistently "being together" sustains our humanity as well as allowing us to constantly deepen our relationships with each other. Therefore, we gather together frequently (weekly or at least every 2 weeks) to celebrate, support each others work in the world, enjoy each other and build the intimacy bonds of deep community. After our personal partner and children, we are each other's first priority. We show up! (see Chapter 36)

We Support Each Other's Need for Solitary Time: Especially as women and men mature into elder hood the need for alone time is essential. We encourage our members to listen to and honor their intuition and knowingness while also expecting clear communication before absence from group gatherings. We make the commitment to communicate regularly.

Our Preferred Age Grouping: For example a "core" community might be mostly over 40 with the main cluster in their 50s, with some in their 60s, 70s & up. Or it might be all young parents with kids in school. Yet, another example may deliberately span at least 3 generations, which includes some younger singles, couples with children and elders.

Membership Sequence Process We establish specific criteria, guidelines and systems by which we admit new members. Candidates pass through a provisional time period during which we get to know each other and mutually determine the appropriateness of the fit. (see Chapter 46)

Group Size: We grow organically and dynamically as a tribal body 15 to 50 people with 150 as the understood maximum size within which we might still contain intimacy. We choose to nourish these close friendships vs. many casual acquaintances. (see Chapter 49)

Gender Safety: We hold a high value on intimacy from the heart between male and female members. Because we want safety for authentic intimacy within our Core Community we require some boundaries and agreements around sexual behavior. To maintain the highest level of trust we consciously avoid secrets, choose transparency and hold strong boundaries around sexuality. (see Chapter 37)

Diversity: We are open to all races, social classes, religions and sexual orientations? We ask, does everyone in our group look like us? Some consider cultural diversity deeply essential to survival and others think homogeneity offers enough interpersonal diversity.

Mutual Activist Support: Because our vision is to build a better and safer world for our children we hold some of our conscious focus on sharing and supporting each others projects. We do this in a deliberate, regular and focused way at every regular meeting.

Governance: We recognize the need to establish some functional leadership or administration within the community. The champion(s) pass on the leadership tasks as soon as it becomes possible. Each community works out the leadership roles, process of decision-making, and operations of the community.

Finances: We know that some monthly assessment will eventually be needed to support the operations of the community. It might be $10 or $20 per month paid in annual amounts of $120 to $240.00. We will elect and trust our administrators to figure out where to use funds as our needs show up.

Leaving Honorably: Because we explored each person's integrity and ability to make a commitment, we do not expect much turnover. However if significant life circumstances change there may be a need to leave or take a break from the group. Because we value transparency we know each other's situation and a need to leave is not likely to be a surprise. This allows anyone to leave honorably and ideally with a heartfelt good-bye ceremony as they go with blessings all around.

Conflict Resolution: We recognize the skillful resolution of conflict as one of the most important skills we can have. We know that many of us have these skills, learned from previous training and/or community situations. We will develop a brief training model so that we all share a similar skill set in the ability to process conflict. (see Chap. 39) If individuals can simply not resolve a conflict themselves they may need mediation by a circle of elders.

Involuntary Exit: If an accountability issue is broken or other incompatibility arises which cannot be successfully mediated by a circle of elders - the membership may ask a person to leave. This might be done by consensus with a "what's best for all" orientation or with a 75% or 66 % of the group deciding to ask someone to leave. If consensus cannot be reached for two meetings at the third there will be a vote and if 75% says out, the matter is settled.

PART 6

COMMITMENTS

*Commitment makes relational intimacy possible,
and relational intimacy deepens commitment,
until there is no difference between commitment
to our own healing and awakening,
and commitment to our intimate relationships.*

Robert Augustus Masters

Chapter 33   Why Commitment

*"Life is too precious to be a spectator sport.
We are no longer merely fans, rooting for the
winning team. We are the team. We are the
grown-ups. Whatever you believe is true,
now is the time to give your respectful,
inquisitive and compassionate self to it."*

-- Vicki Robin

Community starts with Commitment as <u>the</u> essential element! In my 1992 book A Circle of Men, the second chapter is called Commitment and the first line says *"Without commitment the group doesn't work... if the men don't come to "group," it doesn't exist."* And indeed the same is true for community. Think about the groups you are in, some may have unspoken commitments, some none and a rare few an agreement of some sort is made by the members.

The champions determine the commitments for themselves and others to follow. In this section we suggest some commitments that we believe will be useful in holding core communities together. The champions are of course fully free to second-guess anything we suggest and come up with new ones which may work better in each situation.

When we asked what commitments will help a community stay together, the answers we found were:
1. It's essentially personal, we commit to each other.
2. We stay put, we commit to place, not moving.
3. We choose and commit to spend ample time together.
4. We respect and commit to each gender's safety.
5. We commit to our personal integrity & responsibility.
6. We guide each other and commit to resolve conflict.
7. We hold attention on and commit to our long-term community.
8. We commit to support each other's action in the world.

Fear of commitment: We live in a commitment phobic society. We tend to want to keep our "options open" because what if someone better comes along, or we get a call to move or a better job opportunity. Sometimes, one of the unconscious ways that people who are afraid of commitment keep relationships from getting too intimate is by always seeing potential partners or friends as not quite good enough. The cure of course is learning to see thru "good enough" eyes. It opens so many options. Suddenly our partner radiates and our community is filled with these perfectly adequate and actually quite lovable folks.

Commitment is highly related to our community vision and values.

Our goals will come from what we hold dear and are able to imagine as possible. Our vision plus our commitment drives the action that will keep us on track, motivated and able to create what we want.

As you go on to explore some of these commitments in this section in more detail please consider which ones will work best to build a durable base for your long lasting core community.

Some Robert Augustus Masters wisdom on Commitment

Mature commitment is rooted in an integral, well seasoned knowingness.

Real commitment in a relationship cannot be forced.

Don't rush commitment, and don't put it off.

Integrity and commitment are closely linked. Without integrity, there is no real commitment, but only promises and reassurances.

In any commitment, we are making a choice not to make a bunch of other choices; that is, we are embracing a particular set of limitations. This will seem entrapping to the immature, but not to the mature.

Commitment is an open-eyed, ongoing yes to a well-considered choice.

Real commitment is more than meeting another halfway.

Chapter 34   Commitment to Each Other

"Perhaps the fundamental issue in community-building is not physical location or frequency of contact, but rather commitment to establishing and maintaining community."

Carolyn Baker

Community starts with commitment to each other. Whether it is done unconsciously or with thoughtful intention, commitment is community.

In our culture personal commitment normally exists only as an unstated feeling of trust and affection for certain others. Rarely is it an openly stated understanding between friends. Open or not, commitment sustains the bonding of people choosing to be together in one way or the other. We might actually say "I love you" or "I'll cover your back" but just what does that mean? If you were asked if you are committed to your friends, you would say "sure, of course." If the question continued to, "What does that commitment mean?" You might say it means calling them every couple weeks, getting together once in a while or being there for them in some way if they were sick or injured.

It's all good, however there seems to be several specific commitments that we believe will be most needed for stable long-term community. By asking for commitment, we are naming the structure by saying, "this is how it will be in this community!" This is the task of the champions.

Here, we will experiment with saying it with clear intention. Community starts with commitment to each other. Commitment to each other can feel like the scariest and probably the most intimately important part of community building. This level of commitment may seem like a marriage commitment. And indeed this is an apt metaphor. It is not to be taken lightly. We intend a future together.

And sometimes it is a package deal like a blended family. Early on, our friend, Wendy made it clear that her priority is to her kids, then it's the community. And she will be with us as regularly as she can, but if her kids need her or want her, she will be with them. So part of the deal is embracing the children and even grandkids as part of core community. This then provides opportunities for mentors to be chosen and enriching everyone.

Chapter 35   Commitment to Place

The only way to solve the global problem is by local solutions worldwide. I do not believe that there is anything that is purely global. Everything that is global has local roots.

Vandana Shiva

The commitment to place seems so obvious and apparent, yet we need to say it clearly here. If we keep moving, community keeps being broken and will not deeply bond. The model of community we envision in this book is local, **bicycle distance.** Committed to this place, right here. We are suggesting and advocating for physically local community.

Again, let us say the obvious - that being together at the same time in the same place face-to-face allows the trust to build deep community. It might happen by accident over many years, but a shared promise to stay here with each other, makes it so much more possible.

We live in a highly mobile culture, we move too fast. Robert Putnam in his book *Bowling Alone* identifies our propensity to moving as one of the reasons why families, neighborhoods and small towns are long gone as genuine community. The simple truth is that we have to be physically with others to embody the feeling of authentic community.

Our story: Over the last couple years we have reached out to a variety of friends. The ones new in town and especially newly married reached back with eagerness. We bonded, built trust, then the shadows emerged, and so quickly unpleasant divorces, and our sweet friends were gone far away to Nova Scotia and Colorado leaving us with broken hearts.

We are still in touch by phone and Skype, but it isn't the same. We are fully aware of many other variations of community: the extended and virtual communities which all have their value in offering some support and some sense of belonging.

Think of it this way, it takes a certain amount of energy to maintain relationships or we simply forget each other. Those we see every day or once a week will stay in our hearts for many years. Those we contact by phone will stay fresh for a while. We all have limited energy, and we decide which relationships to nurture.

Lots of phone or Skype time will maintain several long-distance friends. A weekly support group will nurture local friends. Perhaps we can do both. We each decide.

We're also painfully aware of how hard it might be to "stay put" for many people who live in big cities and want out. Even suburbs are expected to have major challenges as access to cheap oil limits our transportation options. And those who live in rural country feel isolated by too many miles from others. These days so many people feel edgy and imagine that moving somewhere else is the solution.

If you are truly not "home" yet and your immediate issue is finding that place to which you can make a commitment - **do it now.** Do what ever it takes. Cut your losses and go to where you can become rooted in.

If you are settled where you want to be, find other people also **staying put.** Ask them the obvious question: Are you committed to staying here? Find the people committed to the land, the bio-region, the neighborhood in which you live together. Identify those people staying right there, in that place, choosing to live within bicycle distance of each other by conscious choice. When you do, you have found a candidate.

The catch 22 in all this involves those people who are not sure they are going to stay there in your place. If you build relationship with them, they very well may commit to staying there to be part of the core community. So it becomes a personal call as to where to focus your time and energy.

Chapter 36   Commitment to Time Together

The scarcest resource is not oil, metals, clean air, capital, labor, or technology. It is our willingness to listen to each other and learn from each other and to seek the truth rather than seek to be right.
Donella Meadows

Intimacy and trust: If we have made commitment to each other and to this place we live in perhaps it's time to decide how much time we spend together.

Let us be together every seven days for a few hours. Sounds so easy, people have done this for centuries at church and other social situations. For too many of us today it's almost unthinkable: so, we struggle with the question of just how much time will we actually spend together.

The actual time together is a deeply important feature of any group of people with the intention of intimacy and bonding with each other. I suspect we need to gather together frequently; weekly feels minimal. We simply need the time together to celebrate, work on tasks and support each other's work in the world. It is in the consistency that we consciously enjoy each other and build the intimacy bonds of deep community.

Studies of "feral children" indicates that we are highly social creatures and our complex "humanity" come from intense interpersonal interaction from infancy on. And this need does not stop with becoming "adults" as our growth and individual evolution continues as long as we stay open.

The case has been strongly made that we humans actually need to be with others every seven days or we begin to "forget who we are." Little wonder that people of all the major religions around the world for centuries gather each week. This is the divine evolutionary wisdom of untold generations simply doing what works.

Too Busy: Because our hyper-activity culture often feels addictive, a community with a shared and overarching vision can serve as a way to actually narrow our breadth of commitments. A more limited focus might serve the deeper intentions of our other activities. If we know the depth of our priority commitments we may discover a context for all other activities. If I know what I value the most, all else will find it's place.

For several years I've been reading Carolyn Baker's writing on community. In her new book she suggests from her study of actual situations that:

> "intentional communities and ecovillages that are consciously preparing for collapse, ... a significant amount of time is devoted to community building—sometimes a minimum of three hours a day."

Obviously this seems excessive, however she goes on the say:

> "What many living communities have discovered is that community building requires so much time that its members have extricated themselves from the system of empire to such an extent that they have the time required to devote three or four hours per day to sitting in a circle and processing feelings and making decisions about the community's well being."

Practical suggestions: Ideally each community member commits to being present at full meetings each week or every other week at a minimum. These could be a Sunday or Saturday in the morning, afternoon or evening. To have enough time to not just be a token show-up event we will need 3 to 4 hours minimum. A pot-luck meal of lunch or dinner to share adds that "breaking bread together" family feeling. A restaurant venue probably is not best as it's too impersonal and expensive.

My Group: Ideally each member will commit to being in a small group of 5 to 8 people, which meets every week or at least every other week. (See chapter 38) In my own group we often give each other rides to the airport or go shopping together just to have extra time with each other. And when big work projects come up, we pitch in and it soon becomes fun helping these people we cherish.

Long-term time together: This decision comes as part of the commitment to each other. People do consciously choose to pursue lifelong friendships with each other. They intend their community will be there to care for them, to care for their families and to bury each other when the time comes. Even with such intention we have found it too much of a stretch to think in terms of "forever," given the volatility of our world. After much mutual soul searching, we have committed to each other in our "core community" for a minimum of 3 years, with a lifetime intention. This is a significant conversation and decision for the champions.

Chapter 37   Gender Safety:
Community rooted in Trust and Transparency

Observe the eagle, flying with two wings. One the masculine, the other the feminine and see how it needs both to fly strong.

Cree grandmother, Northern Quebec

We want a community where women and men can live with trust and open hearted transparency. We want healthy relationships with the other gender in which we can feel fully safe and meet some of our love, intimacy and even "snuggle" needs. We all want to be appreciated, nurtured and touched.

Yet the wounding and confusion around sexuality makes even talking authentically about it difficult. In too many cross-gender social relationships the degree of intimacy is severely limited due to the unconscious fear, secrets and shame around sexuality.

We offer here two potential strategies for dealing with this most challenging aspect of bonded community. Both are rooted in transparency even as they range from consciously closed sexuality to fully open sexuality. We do not have the "right" answer, just two practices that we see actually working well. Community devoted to creating a future of co-honoring men and women is possible.

History of abuse: Because we're suggesting a huge social shift, lets look a bit at the impasse. For complex reasons far beyond the scope of this book men have dominated and abused women for far too long. Women have deep cellular memory of being overpowered by rape, degradation and objectification. Women retaliated with subtle, yet powerful skills leaving men with a collective fear of being manipulated, shamed and objectified by women. Men and women have both violated the other gender.

All this covert gender violence continues, as some religions perpetuate the shame and fear around sexuality, equating our original nature with sin. And Madison Avenue is responsible for the gross misuse of "sex" to sell nearly everything in our culture. These are the unsettled waters that men and women swim in. We know that stepping out of this dysfunctional muck would be healthy for us both culturally and individually. Yet, how can we break free from something so pervasive and insidious?

Our research suggests that over recent centuries the intentional communities that remained together had well defined boundaries and agreements around sexuality. The boundaries were understood and agreed to by everyone. In some communities sexuality was very openly shared. Some shared sex with mates only and some allowed absolutely none (until they died out like the Shakers). So, the actual behavior was less important than the clear boundaries. **Clear boundaries work!**

No Secrets: There is much to be said about why boundaries are so important, but to sum it up: **once secrets start, trust leaves** and without trust a community disintegrates. Keeping everything open involves clear agreements and boundaries.

Boundaries that work: For several years we've been part of a deep intimacy community rooted in a simple promise of no sexual acting out with anyone (except primary partners) in the community. People soon get that even unconscious flirting behavior can too often be simply inappropriate, as it invites what we don't want. The clear spoken agreement allows the community a great deal of safety for intimate relationship-learning and physical nurturing. It allows people to stay fully present in relationships, as there is no intention of conquest or seduction.

Such a community seems to require people grounded in significant psychological inner work. They are highly self-aware, mature emotionally and have dealt with inner mother and father wounding. Having lived with my eyes wide open since the sixties, I've seen so many free sexuality experiments fail that I've come to believe in the wisdom of the monogamous cultures over the millennia. And I think this non-sexual boundary also works well for my boomer age group.

If our goal is to create a safe environment for trust and open transparency, how might a non-sexuality agreement serve us? Imagine an agreement like this: "I commit to being non-sexual with every person except my partner, in this community as long as it exists." Did you look for ways out, escape clauses?

The concern we hear most often is "What about single people in the community who fall in love with each other?" This actually happened in our community. When the couple knew they were committed to each other they came to the community to announce that they intended to add sexuality to their love making process. They openly asked for the blessing of the community. A ceremony was thoughtfully prepared and held with a two symbolic arrows ritually broken, symbolizing the vow, and the pieces tied together with ribbons by each of the group members honoring the new bonding. The couple was warmly blessed both for their committed new love and for the integrity with which they handled their agreement around sexuality with the community. A wonderful wedding followed a year later.

In a mature community there will be room for individuals who do come to love each other in a way that calls for sexual intimacy, to bring their change of agreements to the community in an honorable way. The non-sexual agreement is there to serve trust and open hearted loving connection between friends in community without unhealthy predation. Both the agreement and situational flexibility need to be in place for trust to deepen in community. Vows and promises are essential to set a standard of high integrity.

All this should be done together as a community to support each other in the integrity of the commitment. The commitment to being non-sexual is much bigger than between two people, it's the whole community. This promise is likely to be a significant part of each members initiation or commitment ceremony, as it would be done in full community. This is a public promise and commitment to all the people to act with integrity in all relationships.

Open Sexuality: I want to present another dramatically different possibility. A few years ago I met **Ina and Achim from the ZEGG community** which has thrived for 30 years with what in the 60s we called "free love." How they describe it on their beautiful website is: "In the community lovers can open to both the inner and outer movements which love needs to stay alive. When there is trust, love can expand and include more people – this also applies to erotic and sexual love."

Obviously sexuality is a small part of a remarkable social experiment. The name ZEGG means "Centre for Experimental Culture Design" and it's an intentional community, an ecovillage and a seminar center near Berlin in Germany. Early in their history the community residents developed a training called *ZEGG-Forum: Integral community design* (a personal process in a social context) as a powerful tool to create trust and transparency in committed communities. (www.zegg.de)

"ZEGG-Forum integrates individual healing work within the process of building strong community." They do the inner work needed to maintain the high trust to sustain their community. Over the years their training kept evolving and now "incorporates the worldview of Non-violent Communication, the soft exploration of Deep Ecology, the representative work of Family Constellations and the spiritual practice of presence." I'm impressed with what ZEGG has developed and suspect that their training would serve any community, no matter what the boundary agreements they decide upon around sexuality.

Chapter 38   Commitment to a Small Group

Community only really occurs in small groups.
                                                        Cecile Andrews

Personal Support Groups: Besides the larger weekly community gathering we also suggest a smaller personal group. This is fairly easy when people already have a book club or support group they meet with regularly to do inner work. This deeply augments the core community, as it provides the place for adequate "air time" to share and grow consistently. It frees up some energy to be more present, work and play in the larger community gatherings.

This is a simple and astonishingly powerful add-in to our lives. The small groups not only support each person's on-going personal emotional needs, but can focus specifically on inner work or creative energy. For example some people might want a "process group" which is personal growth oriented. Another variety might focus on tasks or co-developing needed social inventions. These groups can be either same sex or mixed gender groups.

In the small personal groups the actual time together is an important feature. We simply need the time together to celebrate, work on tasks and support each other's work in the world. It is in the consistency that we consciously enjoy each other and build the intimacy bonds of deep community. A weekly group has always felt right to me, and I'm often in two separate groups every week.

Some History: Over the last few decades many of us found our first experience of authentic community in a "support group." In the very early 1970s a friend was married with a woman in a women's group. He could see the obvious value and power for her and suggested to me that we form a men's group. To which I responded "What's a men's group?" We figured it out and soon it was one of the most precious parts of my life. It touched my life so much that when the men's movement got rolling I realized that I had learned from my own needs and passion a lot about support groups and had a gift that had to be given. I worked hard writing a book that pushing thru my personal barriers and limitations. In 1992 *A Circle of Men: The Original Manuel for Men's Support Groups* was published. It served men, and also some women, for 15 years and stayed in print until 2007. Now it's a pricy antique on Amazon.

Chapter 39   Resolving Conflict

"The essential dynamics of pseudo-community is conflict-avoidance: true community is conflict-resolving."

Scott Peck

Conflict is a natural and important part of any community. Yet, many of us have not been trained in healthy ways of handling conflict. We live in a dysfunctional swirl of suppression and avoidance until the dam breaks.

When we find the wisdom and courage to welcome conflict and trust our capacity to grow from the heat generated, we know we are in divine service. Carolyn Baker in her book Sacred Demise, says:

> "Since communities are almost always torn apart or dissolved as a result of emotionally-based issues, it is imperative that a commitment to working with feelings (this is deep listening and deep truth telling, in the context of community) be given the same priority as physical survival. Why? Because if emotional issues are not consciously addressed and worked through, they can and will sabotage the community's very existence. What is more, every tribe, every community must develop skills for resolving conflict. Conflict will and should arise. Its absence is, in my opinion, a red flag, signaling glaring dysfunction and seething cauldrons of unspoken feeling and truths that need to be told.
>
> All indigenous cultures at their highpoints skillfully navigated conflict, in fact welcomed it, as a barometer of the communities health. They also developed ever-more creative skills for addressing it compassionately and assertively. Fundamental to addressing conflict in tribal venues is a **council of elders.** Growing up in the tribe, one is taught from birth a profound respect for elders and the importance of deferring to their wisdom. This is not to say that elders are infallible or somehow more than human. Indeed they make mistakes and are rarely known or their charm or congeniality. What enhances their stature is the wisdom they have gained and demonstrated to the community, which does not necessarily supersede the wisdom of other members of the tribe, but can often serve as both an anchor and a compass in navigating conflict."

Thus let us welcome conflict as an opportunity to polish our gifts both individually and as a group. There are many models for resolving conflict.

A Model for Resolving Conflict: For many years in MKP we have used a "clearing" model for dealing with conflicts between men.   Briefly when a man feels hurt, slighted or believes the other is "out of integrity" he calls for a "clearing."   The others offer their attention and sometimes facilitate the process.

It is usually done as a four-step process in which the one who initiates:
1. States what he saw, heard or felt <u>literally</u>. Just as it happened.
2. Tells how he <u>interpreted</u> this behavior. What is the story he made up.
3. Shares how he felt <u>emotionally</u>. Sad, mad, glad, fear or shame.
4. Finally, what he wants. Request of behavior change.

The receiver listens and perhaps feeds back what he heard to make sure the message was received. He may then acknowledge with gratitude the gift of the sender, for taking the time and courage to "clear" and open the relationship to a safer and deeper friendship. There is no defending here, as it's a gift given. The receiver might take some time to share the original intention of the behavior, which had been interpreted in a way which seemed offensive. It's an open exploration of people who care for each other and want to simply understand more deeply.

This model does require some basic training in skills and shared assumptions. First is the ability to separate a **literal observation** from the **interpretation** which is assumed to be a "story I made-up," which may or may not be true. This involves the skill of standing in the "not knowing" as we look for a mutual higher truth, beyond right/wrong thinking. Next comes "emotional literacy" the ability to know and express our emotional feelings. A simple shorthand for these is: sad, mad, glad, fear and shame. Finally the skill of asking clearly for what we want. Sounds easy, but it can be challenging to hold lightly the knowing that we might not get what we want.

The "clearing" begins with the willingness to assume that **it is all about me.** I do this clearing to learn more about me and resolve stuff between us. If we can do this well it bonds us in a variety of ways. It requires the courage to enter the conflict from an open and vulnerable position of self-exploration.

The clearing process is usually a one-on-one situation, sometimes if facing an especially volatile situation it's done with facilitation. This involves a mutually agreed upon person or group as "container holder" for guidance and safety. If this does not work and the "wounded" person does not feel adequate resolution with the "offending" person, the conflict may be called to "community review" often held by the elders. Like a tree a person or organization gets stronger with stress of high wind.

The Total Truth Process is another slightly more complex model people in community might use to break through interpersonal conflict.

Explanation: The reason it is called the total truth is that, often when we're upset, we <u>fail to communicate all our true feelings</u> to the person we're upset with. We get <u>stuck at the level of anger or pain</u> and rarely move past it to emotional completion. Thus it can be difficult to feel close to or comfortable with the other person after such an angry or painful confrontation.

The Total Truth Process can be conducted verbally or in writing. Whichever method one chooses, the goal is to express the anger and hurt, then move toward forgiveness and love. If one participates verbally it is done always with the other person's permission. Begin by expressing the anger, and then move through each stage all the way through to the final stage of love, compassion, and forgiveness.

Feel free to use any example as a prompt to help focus each stage. For the process to be effective, spend an equal amount of time on each of the six stages."

Stages of the Total Truth Process

1. Anger and resentment
Example: I'm angry that...I'm fed up with... I don't like it when…I resent...

2. Hurt
Ex: It hurt me when...I feel disappointed about... I feel sad when…I feel awful about...

3. Fear
Ex: I was afraid that...I'm afraid that...I feel scared when...

4. Remorse, regret, and accountability
Ex: I'm sorry that...I'm sorry for...Please forgive me for...I didn't mean to...

5. Wants
Ex: All I ever want (ed)...I want (ed)...I want you to...I deserve...

6. Love, compassion, forgiveness, and appreciation
Ex: I understand that...I appreciate...I forgive you for...and I forgive myself for...

PART 7

MEMBERSHIP

Where love rules, there is no will to power
and where power predominates,
there love is lacking.
The one is the shadow of the other.
                                                        —Carl Jung

Chapter 40   Finding Members

Where are the people we want in our community? Once the champions have a clear vision, structure and shared values for the community they begin the process of identifying the first candidates to be invited.

Finding members: This progressive process begins with friends we already know and trust. Once the first wave of these close friends who ideally have been known for decades has been brought into this core community as full members then they begin bringing in the next wave of their most trusted friends. This organic process continues until the appropriate size has been reached. Depending on the extent of pre-established friendships this could take from many months to years. Situational urgency could speed up the process.

Doing stuff together: Projects and work and parties, weddings are all ways we share time and get to know others. Look for these opportunities and within the process look for the people you resonate with. Reach out gently.

Who is ready: It seemed so profoundly obvious that everyone wants community that for some time I did not even question it. Yet I encountered enough consistent intense resistance that I actually began to study what was going on. I discovered that people are often not ready for many reasons. Below is a typical story of an innocent response to just asking an obvious qualifying question.

Never even thought of it: Last year I asked Tim and Sarah a solid local couple if they were committed to staying in Ashland. I would describe them as conscious, well networked, bright, competent, spiritual and psychologically healthy. They have lived in Ashland many years, have a son in our local High School and are involved in the Unity Church community.

Their response actually surprised and educated me. They both were instantly clear that they might be "called' to move on. They mentioned a pattern of moving every six to eight years. They did not know where they might go or why, but suspected the call would come. They had no reason to leave Ashland, actually they rather liked it. However at least Tim was clear that he could and would be happy anywhere. It took a few deep breaths for me to hear them, get the sincere truth of what they were speaking, and eventually bless them for sharing their truth about what I call commitment to place.

Only later did I have some insight into the correlation between what they were presenting and the four stages of relationship/community (see Chap. 17). It appeared that they were well evolved in their ability to be highly flexible. Thus their non-restricted, autonomous and independent qualities gave them both the ability and willingness to move anywhere knowing they would be happy. This transcended an older dependency on place as in "stuck in the hometown of parents and extended family."

They were operating out of "stage 3" or co-independent in which they cherish the independence and freedom it affords them in many ways. It took many of us, in our generation, a lot of courage to make this leap and shift away from the stifling codependence in which we saw our parents living.

Several months later I heard that Tim and Sarah had gotten married as part of their commitment to staying in Ashland. Apparently my having just asked the question got them to thinking and talking about the beliefs from which they were operating and somehow they realized that they could indeed be committed to place and indeed each other as part of an even more mature process.

This appears to reflect another stage in choosing where and how we live. Perhaps we are becoming both mature and autonomous enough to imagine **"choosing attachment"** as even a better way. If we able to imagine such a possibility, perhaps we can then ask a few friends like Tim and Sarah to consider "Where do you really want to be?" and maybe even "What do you really want?" This might quickly lead to asking them selves "How might I get what I really want?" They just might open their own door to community.

Finding the "right" community: As stated earlier from my MKP–I–group observations over the years our best friends tend to be those with whom we spend the most time, who live close by, the ones we actually see and hang-out with often. So ask, who is near-by you that you might want to be friends with, time to sort them out.

Some sage advice from a little book for single women some years ago called The Good Enough Man essentially suggested that if a woman wanted to stay single forever, wait for Mr. Perfect, or she might look at the man in front of her and ask "Is he good enough?" and let your love flow. It is the same with community, within a few square miles are thousands, literally thousands of people many of whom are plenty good enough. In this section lets look at the sorting process of just how do we choose or not choose our community.

Chapter 41 Do I Have the right to Choose?

The Biggest Challenge: The single most controversial issue I have encountered in my years of exploration and conversation about how to build community is around who is "in" and who is "out." People ask; "Do I have a right to pick and choose who I want in my community?" or "Is it really OK to <u>select</u> the community members?" Because "selecting members" is such a loaded issue I want to devote a chapter to grappling with the question.

Early wounding: Many of us carry painful memories of rejection or abandonment from having been infants left alone, babies left with nannies or day care. As children we were teased, bullied or simply excluded from the "in-crowd." In grade school or high school the "in-out" dynamic often hurt and caused us to close down. The "black ball" I got which excluded me from a fraternity in my sophomore year of college, still stings. Most of us still smart from some "exclusion wounds" as we grew up. This may have led to what in spiral dynamics is called the "mean green meme" which means dysfunctional hyper-inclusivity. An ethic has evolved which demands that everyone be included. I suggest that this inclusivity is actually very important in "bridging" communities and needs to be compassionately transcended in "bonding" communities.

Making distinctions: Choosing long term bonding community consciously may be an entirely new idea for many of us. Because it's not related to an established organization (religion, fraternal club or workplace) it requires much higher intention and awareness. To actually deliberately choose people for a personal community of commitment is a new social phenomenon.

No choice: Some people believe from study or intuitive knowing that they may not discriminate as to who is in their community. They feel morally bound to not allow themselves a "right" to choose, so to be in integrity they may not choose. Some people choose to live with whoever shows up in their life and relish the challenge. They might say "The doors are wide open, let's see who shows up and enjoy learning how we deal with each other."

Choosing people for one-time events: We choose all the time with the people we have over for dinner, invite to a party or a wedding. We select the ones who will be the most fun or highest status, invite them and see how it plays out. We keep it always flexible and open which works fine, it just does not build intimacy very quickly if ever.

Conscious awareness of diversity issues: Some of us have learned to be aware of and highly sensitive to prejudice or discrimination around race, gender and sexual preference. I deeply support this inclusive way of holding all fellow humans

Choosing community: I see this as a new phenomenon, because it opens a field of possible human social relationships not previously known. Here we make inclusion decisions consciously in the interest of the building intimate community. As the purpose of a group is focused around bonding (vs. bridging) it will probably be best to choose members carefully.

Some Advice: For those of us who can imagine that we have a right or even a duty to choose, let me share with you from the work of Dianna Leafe Christian who served as editor of Communities Magazine for 15 years and author of two books on Ecovillages and intentional communities. She has heard all the stories and has powerful advice;

From *Creating A Life Together,* Chapter 18 called: Selecting People To Join You:

> Accepting someone into your already established community who is not aligned with your vision and values, or who triggers strong reservations, doesn't work. It can potentially lead to spending hours of meeting time on conflicts that leave everyone draining and exhausted or worse, to community breakup. And, because people project so much idealism onto community, we tend to make the same kind of mistakes choosing community mates as we do when choosing a lover: leaping before we look, projecting idealized archetype onto ordinary folks, refusing to pay attention to telltale signs.
>
> The antidote is to put in place **a well-designed process for accepting and integrating new members and screening out those who don't resonate** with your group. Since community living involves getting along well with others, you will want to select people whose lives demonstrate they can do this. Ideally, you'll select for emotional maturity and self-esteem.
>
> **Not having a membership selection process can be heartbreaking source of structural conflict later on.**

Chapter 42   Selecting Members

As suggested in the previous chapter, you will probably want to be highly selective in this part of your lives. The people whom you choose to include in your core community will ideally be the most resonant, geographically stable and compatible. These are the ones in whom we want to invest our time and love as they will likely become long-term friends. Again it is important to say that our intention is to build a strong "bonded" community as a base to give our "bridging" community gifts ever more fully. (see Chapter 5) And let me reaffirm that these selection criteria would ideally be rooted in the vision and values and of each core community.

Qualities and Criteria: Once the champions have developed their clear vision and values they may have speculated a bit as to whom they might invite. They now need to refine the criteria for selection because it will become a future reference for this core community.   Below are some qualities and criteria you may want to consider as a guide in your selection process:

Psychological Maturity: We suggest choosing people who have done adequate psychological inner work.   They will be emotionally aware enough and have enough psychic strength to know their wounded child complexes ("pain body" - "shadow").   They are self aware enough to have internalized values which they hold as "who they are" which is integrated with a view of healthy society. They are socially aware enough to know that people in community will disagree and they have the capacity to resolve these conflicts to the benefit of all. They are courageous and transparent enough to know that intimacy grows from the risk of self revelation and they know how to reach out in this way.
Thus, each person has integrity, strong personal accountability, conflict resolution and intimacy skills.

Spiritual Maturity: Unless your religious preference is highly focused you will want to invite people who have done "adequate" spiritual inner work. You will likely want people who have engaged in their own search for the divine and found a satisfactory path, which guides their life. Ideally they each hold their best understanding of the sacred and do not impose it on anyone else. This usually reflects the "golden rule" and human connectedness.

Diversity Welcome: It needs to be stated that the psychological, social and spiritual specifications in no way excludes any ethnic, religious, sexual orientation or racial differences. The richness here is the deliberate choice of diverse people for a core community, which can enhance growth potential in very dynamic ways. Some say that this is <u>the</u> essential quality for survival.

Gender Safety: If we hold a high value on connecting deeply from the heart between women and men within our community we want safety for authentic intimacy. Because trust is essential we are aware of the severe disruption possible with-in community due to inappropriate or predatory sexual acting out.
Therefore we bring this sexual part of our humanity out of shadow into our collective light. This will allow us to establish some boundaries and agreements around appropriate and "safe" sexual behavior. (see Chapter 37)

Couples: Do they come in separately or as a couple? Because of the trust and intimacy couples share, they would likely consider their relationship to be part of the community process. Observe how durable or stable the relationship appears to be. We've observed that just the idea of "community" can cause an already fragile couple to break up. Sometimes one is ready and feels OK joining without his/her partner, who may join later, or not.
Better to address this before the couple joins as serious questions may arise if a couple within a community splits up. How does the community deal with mixed loyalties? Who stays in and who is out – or can both stay in? Probably their separation needs to be open to the whole community as the decision affects the whole. Because these are very real and legitimate considerations, this process should be spelled out in agreements ahead at time.

State of the World Awareness: It seems wise to know and understand deeply what is currently happening environmentally, economically and socio-politically in the world. These concerns feel integral to the creation of this core community.

Commitment to Taking Action: Recognizing the nature of the times, you may feel called to use your awareness, skills and creativity to serve the cultural transformation each in your own way. Because this is a major intent of this book, we suggest that communities actively support each other's "action in the world." This can embody and enhance the natural ability to respond creatively to change.

Chapter 43   Preparing Ourselves to Invite

Self preparation: Before we offer our gift and our invitation it's appropriate to do some inner self investigation. Am I ready? Can I reach out and offer my gift and truly accept either a yes or no answer? To truly love someone involves truly loving ourselves. If I do not love and accept me -just as I am with wounds and potential- I cannot really love you. Thus when I/we reach out in love it's deeply personal and like any lover, there's a risk of no reciprocity – love not returned. Am I ready to take that chance with my heart open?

A <u>Personal</u> Invitation: Skills I might need.

1.   Knowing myself as the "gift" I offer you my gifts: The "gift" is who we are. We humans are good, loving, compassionate creatures. We live to give and serve. Granted this has been grotesquely distorted by our pathological culture. However, essentially we are by nature wonderful, giving beings.

2.   Knowing how to say "I Need You": I invite you to say it with me "I need you." How did it feel? Now think of someone close to you, focus and say it again "I need you." Feeling check! Again, another person: "I need you." Take it out a little further (do not turn the page yet). Please actually do this before reading on by just imagining saying it to 3 specific people, one at a time, waiting for an inner reaction and note your feelings.

(Personal story) I can tell you this "I need you exercise" was very difficult for me. It felt vulnerable. It felt like a declaration of love. I felt exposed. I felt touched, tears on the ready and scared. This violated something about my feeling safe, like an independent, self-sufficient guy. I had learned to not really need anyone even though my heart yearned for connection. It's really all I wanted. What else is there?

Perhaps "meaningful work" but that is all. Life is pretty simple really. So if I were to focus the rest of my life achieving just these two things what might I do? I might give my attention to love and work. And when I focus my attention on love and work I discover what I have or do not have. This allows me to notice where I might put my energy if I am to get what I really want.

3.   Knowing how to say "I invite you": Here is a suggested example of how to make an invitation, which might include giving someone this book. "Because I am interested in you as a member of my gift community, I give you this book/these chapters. It shows how we all live in our own place and gather together regularly. If you are interested I want to share some details of the vision of a local community I'm exploring. Let's discuss the possibility."

Our core gift community members joke that our process is like dating – we go steady, then after dating for awhile we get engaged and somehow the initiation feels strangely like marriage vows.

4.   **Knowing what I mean by community:** A brief summary as it might be shared. "I want to share about what I call "my core community" because it is the one I'm most committed to. I'd still have plenty of acquaintances but one deep core community. It would develop out of the people I already know or people my friends know that we mutually trust. We check each other out and commit to each other. We meet often, like every week and develop the intimacy of family. Indeed it is a family of choice."

"I've thought about how long we might be together. I have this vision of a community that stays together for a long time. I want to know that they will be there to care for me, perhaps bury me when my time comes as I will be there for them. That's what I want, how about you?"

"Does this sound like something you are interested in? Ok, may I share some specific information, so that you can make a clear decision? We'll start with values and if you share them we've got an important personal and spiritual base. Then we can look at a structure that might work to hold us together at the functional level."

5.   **Knowing your core values and commitments:** You may want to start with some basic core values presented here that resonate well with you. If they feel congruent with who you are they form a shared vision of what you want together with others. Do you feel ready to share your values? (some examples)
    Commit to each other: Choosing the people we want.
    Commit to place: Choosing to live physically close to each other.
    Co-create new community: Building it together.
    Weaving a mutual safety net: Taking care of each other in these times.
    Conscious culture: Being part of a healing process of human sustainability.

6.   **Communicating how it might work:** When you feel ready to offer an invitation you might offer some context, sucha as; "After decades of trial and error there seems to be a model which just might work to build a stable, safe, long term, bonded community. We start with small bonded friendship groups, so that as we

119

grow in size, much safety and trust is already in place. We want to be able to have transparency and authenticity skills so that we can trust beyond a few close friends into a much larger community. Please know that this is an invitation into a process which may or may not feel right to you. Let's explore as to how we might play and work together with a number of people for years to come." Ask: "How does it all sound so far?"

7.   **Be able to accept either a "Yes" or "No" answer:** Sometimes our fear of rejection, rooted in an old invisible "trust issue" can cause us to avoid asking for the community we want. To deal with this possibility do some role-play either inside or out loud of hearing and receiving a "no" from a good friend. Experience the feeling and let it be OK. Bless yourself for your courage in asking and trust that even this friend may simply not be ready to make the subtle yet powerful sacrifices needed to make a commitment to community.

We have been blessed with friends saying "yes" to our invitation. We have also shared a nice dinner with favorite friends as we invited them to explore our core community as possible members, only to hear them sincerely tell us "Thank you Bill and Zoe for the lovely invitation, but we are feeling called to another adventure in another place. It has been our dream for so long, we just have to follow it." We take a deep breath, thank them for considering our offer, pledge to hold them in our hearts, as we each get on with our lives. We feel some sadness that these sweet ones will not be as close as we had hoped, and trust that they know what is right for them.

Chapter 44   Inviting & Sponsoring

We become a "sponsor" the moment we invite our potential "best friends" into a possibility, a vision of something new.   Inviting someone into your core community with long term intention is very personal like saying "I see you," "I need you" or "I feel love for you." We offer the gift of our hearts, our time, our loyalty and trust.   We reach out knowing our feelings may not be reciprocated. This willingness to be rejected is such a loving process.   So, we suggest some preparation of those you intend to invite.

Candidate preparation: Before the invitation we want to offer some guidelines to appropriately prepare your friends.   Ask, are my candidates ready, informed, interested and feeling safe enough to proceed?   Said another way, are they **receptive, prepared and consenting?**

Receptivity: We might be well advised to do what in the business world is called "qualify the buyer" to find out if they are really interested and can really afford what we have to offer.   How this might show up here is to offer enough information (perhaps this book or chapters on the vision and structure) so that he/she/they can opt out even before the conversation and invitation.   There may be personal circumstances or deep unconscious inner resistance that simply cannot be seen from the outside.   There must be plenty of "permission" for people to honor their own feelings and life choices.

Preparation: We let our friends know that we will be inviting them to a conversation in which they will be invited to consider a large and significant possibility.   They know this vision will involve making some big commitments to place and time.   They are informed, having read the "book." They know the structure and possibility toward which we are working.   Fully aware of both promise and peril, we are prepared to touch hearts and deepen the invitation.

Permission: We want to offer transparency and reciprocity to candidates so they know who and what this invitation truly involves.   He/she/they should have all documents available to them, including permission to check out background of anyone asking for this intimate connection with them.   Because I am going to ask for permission to do that with him, I might ask if he would like to "check me out" – even insist on it.   These are like early entrance "gates" in which we discover our mutual resonance, or not.

We offer our gift: When I know they are receptive, feel prepared and safe enough with me to tell their truth, I invite them. In my invitation I give my love, time, loyalty and trust.

Yes or No: If the vision, values and structure feels good and workable; if it's aligned and empowering, they will say YES. We then may proceed with the process. If the values feel contrary or too constricting and the structure feels too rigid, too big or too small, they will say NO or not yet.

If No: If my gifts are not received or if she/he chooses to not pursue this community, so be it. The gift of my love, time, loyalty and trust still stands whether this person chooses to join this committed community or not.

If Yes: Once the invitation has been accepted, there is a commitment set between the inviter (now "sponsor") and the candidate, saying "I commit to guide and support you through the community initiatory process."

Authentic invitation: This seems too obvious, but it has to be said. It's always an invitation, and needs to be felt as such. We are either together because we want to be there or there is some coercion in which someone is being forced or tricked into doing something that they really do not want. Unfortunately, there are millions of examples of churches and quasi-churches that operate as cults in the way they appear to invite yet have subtle "hooks" to "reel em in." So both the one invited and the one doing the inviting needs to be clear on the open flow and true freedom of an authentic "invitation."

Presumption of a personal history: The examples above assume the sponsor has known this person for some years and have shared considerable time and tasks. A trust base has already been established. Local "old timers" actually know each other and who to trust or not trust. When someone is new in town and there is no history or in-depth knowing of them as friends or neighbors, it suggests the need for caution. Here serious vetting is a challenging and very important process. Which leads to the next chapter on how we might do this in a good way.

Chapter 45   Greatest Caution: Vampires

This title may sound trite, but the intent is profound as you will see. I was ambivalent about putting this chapter in, but several of my friends, said YES, it's important information not just for core communities but in broader society and even in making sense of the larger world. This is an uncomfortable conversation about psychopaths. Psychologists would use a more current clinical designation such as Narcissistic Personality Disorder (NPD).

Swami Beyondananda calls such people "sociopathogins" and notes that if they get into to body politic they are toxic. The same is true for community. Most of us assume everyone is a lot like us, and we tend to be very trusting, which is a good quality, however it can make us vulnerable to "them."

Like millions of other I have had direct and painful experience with this type of human. I was stunned and confused. How could a man who called me brother do this to me, treat me this way? As a psychotherapist I had access to the books and seminars to study the NPD in some depth. I cover this briefly in Chapter 51 as I began a process of educating others about "them."

"They" are often hard to talk about, especially for people who have been wounded by such a person. I'm aware that there is some danger here of getting into "us vs. them" thinking.   However, the value is in learning to trust our intuition and knowing what to look for. It's an early warning system that can save much pain. Perhaps we can think of this as part of our conscious boundary setting, that part of our emotional and intelligent self that serves as our inner social immune system.

The intention here is keeping your community safe because "they" are sometimes very hard to spot. Learn the material below and always look for patterns. This is the reason for the membership cautions of spending enough time with candidates and knowing everyone's history.

Context: Every ten years psychiatrists reevaluate and rename psychopathologies in a book called the *Diagnostic and Statistical Manual of Mental Disorders*. The classification now called the Anti-Social Personality Disorder was previously designated as the Anti-Social Character Disorder, which followed the Sociopath which was preceded by Psychopath. For centuries, before we had any clinical language, this very same type of human was known around the world and in most languages by the archetypal name "Vampire."

Human Nature: I believe that we humans are basically good, kind, compassionate and loving beings. And I believe we need to be able to identify that small percentage of humans who function against their own human nature. The rest of us tend to project our essential goodness on all other people. The failure to make this discrimination has led to much of the pain in the world.

Look Inside: We all have some vampire in us. We are animals and we must kill to live. We must predate on something, from an asparagus to a big-eyed cow. We all have some propensity and qualities of the vampire in us. However, some humans grow up profoundly narcissistically wounded in ways that allow vampiric predation to become the primary, driving part of who they are. Approximately 2% of the population fits this identity yet they are responsible for 80% of the pain in the world.

Vampire Spotting 101: Let's look at some of the specific behavioral characteristics that define the unredeemed charismatic vampire. Astoundingly, just about every one of them will exhibit most if not all of these traits:

1. Glib and persuasive
2. Highly impulsive, restless, and easily bored, needing constant stimulation
3. Practiced at using protestations of love and devotion to get what he wants
4. Without feelings of guilt or anxiety
5. Full of fake repentance and promises to do better when caught lying
6. Often presenting business schemes that will return a large payoff if they can just get xxx dollars from you to get him started
7. Totally lacking in conscience
8. Vague and inconsistent about their past
9. Unable to learn from experience and always blaming others for their failures
10. Unable to bond closely, cheating repeatedly on their partners
11. Insistent on unconditional support and understanding, meeting any questioning with accusations that you are untrusting and unloving.

(look at the first five items and you can see how one like this might be highly attractive - until ....)

No allegiance to truth: Vampires lie with such inner certainty that you often feel an emotional consistency. This sets you up in various ways. We call this a "con game" in which they gain your <u>con</u>fidence. Once they have your trust they can manipulate you very easily. Most of us want and tend to trust others, so there are some "vampire" behaviors it would be wise to be aware of.

Learning to "feel" them: It requires being able to trust your intuition to detect vampires in your presence. Often they charm us brilliantly, so we need to be able to "feel" them. You detect something is wrong and don't know quite what it is. You feel a little crazy after you have been with one. Your reality feels strange, uncertain, confused, and it's not an accident. You intuitively know, but talk yourself out of it, with their help of course.

Look at what they do: A great prophet once said, "By their deeds shall they be known." Make a judgment based on what a person does, or doesn't do, not by what they say or convincingly suggest.

Live in the dark: Vampires hate the light of day. They operate in the dark of night. They do not want to be seen. Consciously or unconsciously, they do not want us to know how they suck our life energy. Everything is secret, and accountability is always avoided.

Vampires as shapeshifters seem to know when they are about to get busted and will immediately change and give you whatever they have promised (the hook), or what you want. They know how to be whoever you need them to be, so they can get from you what they want.

Patterns, Patterns, Patterns!!! Vampires shape-shift, live in shadows, often lie with a very straight face, even a very sincere face. To spot one, you must notice patterns. Like after a while, stuff just does not add up. Or you discover in a conversation that someone else observed the same behavior pattern of lies. A pattern has begun to emerge and sometimes you can't see the patterns for months or years.

Vampires set up no-win situations. If you tell, you lose and if you don't tell, you lose. He has set up a double bind which forces you to play at his level. You need to be able to access an awareness place where he can't touch you. Holding the archetypal reality, seeing this being as living out his call/karma may enable you to love him through it.

What, me, vampire? Very slippery creatures. Because they live in denial, they do not know that they are vampires. If you ask one, he'll tell you he's a perfectly nice guy like everyone else. They cannot see their own behavior as any different from others. They honestly do not understand what the consequences of their behavior might mean to others. The self-focused, narcissistic wound runs so deep that they often cannot feel the pain of others. And paradoxically, they do have a very keen sense of the pain in others to the extent that they can exploit it as weakness for their own profit or self-aggrandizement.

Envy is a vampire's middle name: You can feel someone as a vampire when the envy just oozes off of them. When such a person envies what you have as a personal quality, recognizing it does not exist in him and knowing it probably never will, he will try to destroy you. We see this happen on a personal level in simple everyday interactions in which one person will "put down" another to "feel a little bit better about themselves." They want to hurt someone who has what they want. In adolescent cultures it happens often, yet it still hurts and it feels icky even to be in the presence of such an interaction.

On a larger, historic-political level we can see tragic examples of this envy motivated behavior. When "explorers" came to the new world they encountered native peoples who they recognized as having "soul" which they no longer felt in themselves. So they maimed and killed the innocent indigenous peoples. They could not steal their souls, so they had to annihilate them.

Types of Predation: The vampire might suck our life energy emotionally, sexually or financially. On a small level he/she might suck up our time and attention, however with political and financial power they might suck vast amounts of money out of an entire country.

Push into Power: Because the vampire experiences himself as already dead (he has no connection with his inner essence), he has nothing to lose, so has little or no fear. When he moves aggressively into organizations, those with sensitivity feel him and will wisely step aside. Unfortunately, this allows this toxic energy to advance incrementally into places of power where it hides at the top by controlling everything with little or no accountability to anyone.

The charismatic vampire will enroll you in his reality: We might call this "biting" us, which is convincing us that his way of being in the world is the way to be. Once bitten we tend to . . . duh . . . act like vampires. This may sound obvious and funny but imagine that they were very wealthy and powerful and wanted the whole world to think like them so they could feel good about who they are. We would probably have something like our modern media propaganda system owned and operated by a very small percent of citizens who designed it to perpetuate a worldview, which serves mostly them.

Note: It may be worth noting that over the last few decades the "vampire" has showed up in thousands of books, TV shows and films. There is a huge "market" for this material and I suggest that it may be our unconscious way of trying to understand and perhaps heal this very shadowy energy so pervasive in our culture.

Chapter 46   Membership Gates

By "Gates" we mean the stages or thresholds one passes through to gain entry as a member into a community. If we truly want to check each other out before making a commitment, this represents some of the structures we might use.

We use the most straight forward, clear language without "shop-talk or group-speak" for the titles and stages of this process. Below is a sample of a process sequence you might choose to use. Each gate has a rationale as to why we might do it this way.

The "Core Community" Membership Process:
The step-by-step progression through:
The **"3 Gates of Initiation"** into Core Community (CC).
Each stage has: **The Gate, The Process & The Rationale**

#1   THE INVITATION, APPLICATION & ACCEPTANCE

The Gate: Gate #1 is crossed when a person accepts the sponsor's invitation, completes and submits the BASIC INFORMATION & APPLICATION (BIA) which get checked out and approved by the full membership with a decision to bless the candidate on to PROVISIONAL MEMBER (PM) status.

The Process: Each candidate must be invited in by a sponsor who knows him/her well. This begins with the sponsor providing basic information and education about the CC. When a candidate knows enough about the CC and accepts the invitation the BIA form is offered. If/when it is completed the sponsor brings the name of his/her applicant seeking membership to a meeting. Here the sponsor provides the BIA Form as hard copies and speaks for the applicant, providing some basic introduction and information for those that do not know him/her. Concerns will be directed to the sponsor. If fully approved and accepted the applicant becomes a "candidate" and we move to the second gate.

Rationale: The sponsor demonstrates his/her commitment to a candidate by being willing to guide the candidate thru the challenging 3-gate process. This devotion begins with educating him/her sufficiently to know what to expect. The sponsor must honestly "read" the intentional energy of the candidate, not talk him/her into it. We want each person's own clear intention and desire, not a half-hearted, tentative energy.

The sponsor demonstrates his/her commitment to the CC by using this process as an opportunity for the "due diligence" of checking out the applicant before formally proposing him/her to the CC membership. A good fit and compatibility may likely be seen in the way these questions are answered. This will demonstrate a person's gifts and readiness to bring them to the CC.

The BIA Form is also designed as an EARLY SCREEN, as this deliberately short form is designed to allow the CC to:

1. Uncover pre-candidates shadows early in the process. Those who know they will not do well given such scrutiny, especially on the background check, may bow out gracefully with minimum negative impact on themselves or the CC. We want to see a demonstration of courage and a willingness to be vulnerable to judgment knowing they may be turned down, since this clearly suggests strong intention. Also by going thru this process the candidate learns how thoroughly each of us has also been checked out for safety and intimacy.

2. Access the broad wisdom of the community early in the process. Because members have been in the same neighborhood for some time we use the experience of the established networks who know each other from simply being "around town" for a long time. Each member will likely have some personal take on the integrity, values, readiness and maturity of applicants. Those who know this person from a negative experience (red flags) may weigh-in with concerns before we go too far into the process. We also honor each other's experience and judgments as to how well a person will fit in our "core community."

OBJECTIONS: If anyone has considerations or objections, the sponsor might get new information and take another look at the candidate herself or do what ever it takes to get approval from everyone. This may mean arranging conversations for trust building or facilitating conflict resolutions processes.

DECISION: Eventually a decision will be made by the membership body to bless the candidate on to Provisional Membership status or not. If the candidate is turned down it becomes the task of the sponsor to let the person know that it has not worked out for him/her to continue the process.

#2. PROVISIONAL MEMBERSHIP STATUS:

The Gate: Gate #2 is crossed at the end of the allotted time of provisional status.

The Process: When full approval is granted the candidate is invited into a collaborative conversation. Because real commitment is an organic process, selected members and the candidate decide together how long it might take for the unfolding and ripening as we get closer and closer to knowing and trusting each other. The weeks or months or years everyone decides upon is duly recorded and the candidate is welcomed and initiated into Provisional Membership (PM).

Note: Classically, this level of status will run between 3 and 6 months (special note: Early on, this timing may be shortened by founders who already know and trust each other deeply as old established friends).

PMs learn by being part of the CC, here they practice the established community norms, structure, gender safety, intimacy and share their "sacred work". Here they "get fully involved." The PM status carries all the delights and responsibilities of membership, but not the right to make decisions or bring in new members.

Rationale: Here the candidate is invited to fully step into the community and expected to "show up." It is a demonstration of intent through action. This mutually established PM pre-set time together becomes a long mutual learning and "interview" during which we truly "view-each-other." As a long "initiation" this process is designed as an orientation and preparation to become a full member.

3. FINAL INTERVIEW, INITIATION & WELCOME:

The Gate: Gate #3 involves completing the interview with mutual agreement and final OK by the entire Core Community and a classic initiation.

The Process: When the specified provisional time is reached, notice will be sent to all members to be consider the candidate one final time. Any feedback is forwarded to the "elders" (probably the same team who did the PM interview) who will conduct an interview with the PM. The interview is about discovering mutual agreement that sufficient knowing, trusting and intimacy is shared between PM&CC and CC&PM. This conversation might lead to a mutual Yes," "no" or a "not-yet." And if accepted he/she will be invited to be initiated into the Core Community.

INITIATION will be an opportunity for the individual to surrender into the collective body. This ego transcendent process is a liminal experience of joyous unfolding.

THE WELCOME is the formal induction into the community as a full member, at a full meeting. The welcome ceremony is a time of celebration, blessing, honoring and receiving.

Rationale: This is the final decision point and last time for members to express doubts based this time on actually getting to know and work with the candidate over several months. It should be pretty obvious if this candidate feels like a member. Therefore this needs to be taken very seriously as it is the last opportunity to block admission. At this point it is very personal and needs to be done with fierce honesty. The actual interview is intended as an intimate shared process between peers who are making a mutual decision based on time and experiences together. Members with specific concerns are consulted or invited into the interview.

The initiation of the candidate is ideally more than ceremonial ritual. The ordeal of submission (not by abuse or humiliation) is ego-transcendent work in which one "becomes the community."

Chapter 47   Basic Information & Application Form

(This is designed as a model to be adapted and used for individual situations.)

Core Community (CC)

Note: <u>CONFIDENTIALITY</u>, THE COMPLETED FORM WILL BE SHARED ONLY WITH FULL MEMBERS OF OUR CORE COMMUNITY and ONLY AS HARD COPY–NOT E-MAIL.

<u>Basic Information & Application Form</u>:

This document is designed to gather some basic understanding about you & how you see your part in our Core Community and to formally **register** your **request** to enter the membership process.

Legal name: _____ Date: _____

Name you like to be called (if different) _____ Age: ____

Current address: _____

Phone: _____ Email: _____

CC Sponsor: _____ Relationship _____

Part I. Your Understanding of our Core Community:
Please share, in your own words what attracts you to our CC:

Part II. Emotional and Spiritual Well-Being:
Please tell us about any psychotherapy, trainings, emotional healing and/or spiritual work you have experienced and how that might work with our CC.

Part III. Family &/or Lifestyle:
Do you have a significant love relationship now? If so, please tell us about how long you've been together & if your partner wants to join you in this CC.

Part IV. History and credibility:
Would you please write up your life history in a few pages for us to know your history. We would also like your permission to do a background check and contact references, both from long ago and more current, with whom you would be willing to allow us to consult.

Part V. Your Contribution to our Core Community:
What would you see yourself contributing to this **CC**?

I _____ am aware of the **"3 Gates"** of membership process, which includes this **Application, Provisional Membership status and Final Interview Initiation** required before full membership. Therefore, as I choose to make myself available to this process, I hereby request consent to continue the Core Community membership process._

Signed: _____ **Date:** _____

Thank you for completing your Application and sharing this personal Information.

Chapter 48   Initiation in Integrity

To have initiations again we'd have to find a way to bring this banished indigenous soul back home to us and we would have to have communities worth coming home to.   Martin Prechtel

Martin Prechtel goes on to say:
> "For me, true initiation would be impossible until the modern world surrenders to the grief of it origins and seeks a true comprehension of the sacred. A tangible relationship with the divine must be found: a relationship to ritual that actively feeds the invisible forces behind all this visible life."

What he calls "true initiation" appears to involve both relationship with and surrender to the divine or invisible forces. He also invites us to feel the grief of our separation from and damage done to the earth. The words "earth" and "heart" have the same letters. In this metaphor we see that as earth dies, heart dies, and as heart dies, mother earth dies.

True initiation must enter this "lodge of the heart" or what is also called "liminal space." This "threshold" cannot be forced, only held open and with enough good will or love it may show up like a delicious fog. How we enter that "lodge" in an authentic way is a challenge, as we can not just borrow ritual processes from cultures that still have "indigenous soul" Perhaps we start with what we personally know. Many of us value personal integrity.

What is Integrity? For the human being "integrity" refers to having our "parts" working together or in alignment. On a psychological level if there is part of us that is "out of integrity" it means that some part is running contrary to the rest of the "self." This can be seen most simply as a "lie" which by definition is not "true" to the rest of the story. Thus one who lies is seen as "out of integrity" with the community. That person is acting contrary to the values of the rest of the community. Thus an initiation may represent the ritual promise to be "in integrity" with one's commitments to community values.

Some Suggestions for Initiations:

Integrity: Each candidate is invited to present as a "woman/man of integrity" who stands for values of our community. In such declaration we set a formal standard.

It then becomes the promise against which he/she can henceforth be held accountable and responsible. Therefore, a commitment made in this community carries the weight of each person's declaration of integrity which invites observation of a person's behavior in the context of who he/she declares him/her self to be. This serves both the community and the individual as self-correcting organisms.

This may seem overly simple and obvious, however painful experience suggests that if we fail to state our values and intentions clearly it does not allow real accountability. Without clear boundaries the slippery ones can slide thru the cracks in the assumptions of our disconnected culture.

Commitment: As we have suggested many times in this book, without commitment community of any duration is not likely to happen. Therefore it seems obvious that the initiation, the beginning of a person's permanent status into core community as a full member, would involve a formal declaration of commitment.

Earth-Heart context: Imagine the physical and psychic space in which integrity and commitment declarations might be spoken truly from the heart. What setting or energy would be most conducive to accessing the heart? Sunrise on Sunday morning by the creek, or in the park works for me. I imagine feeling fresh and alert with the cool wet grass between my toes. Grounded and ready I give my word as to my intention with this cherished group of people.

Trust yourself, trust the Universe. To be authentic, perhaps each of us simply needs to make the ritual our own by using the ways we know best to enter the open heart from which to speak our truth. The initiation might well be a collaborative co-creation between the current members and the new ones just entering. This will ideally become the "liminal space" as a transcendent threshold in which magic happens. It cannot be created deliberately, only held in receptive hearts. Divine magic comes when It is ready.

Our own experience: In the initiations we have done bringing in "provisional" members and full members, we take some very basic steps. First we prepare ourselves with our intention to hold authentic "sacred space." We set the room ahead of time with candles, flowers, music and proper seating. Sometime if appropriate we prepare food to be shared before or after the ritual ceremony.

When the candidates arrive we greet them in a formal ritual way such as smudging with cedar or sage smoke, then escort them to a specific seat. These are simple things, which are distinctly out of the ordinary and therefore take on significance which focuses attention. We then direct attention to important aspects of what makes us unique together.

Our shared values and commitment to each other are the obvious points of focus. We ceremonially review the values (see chap. 31) by holding a card with each value artistically displayed. A member reads the value and comments on what it means. It is passed to the initiate who tells how she holds it and perhaps relates a personal challenge she faced regarding this value in her life.

As founders or champions of our community Zoe and I also needed to be initiated by the first three full members. I can't tell you exactly what happened, but you might imaging being met at the car, escorted to a formal greeter, where we were blindfolded and led to a secret place. We were met by song, blessings, and poetry as the late afternoon sunlight blended thru the trees and the creek gurgled close by. The vows felt strangely and wonderfully like a marriage, reassuring and a little daunting, warmly received. It was formal ceremony with heart.

Later at the house we renewed our commitment to our values with our ceremonial candle holder, with just the right number of candles. Then the ritual art piece was introduced with copper coils, which we garnished with carefully chose beads. Suddenly it became the symbolic interlocking of our little community. We just make it all up with loving intention. Our hearts lead us to what our heads want and we mark it with sacred symbols and ritual, which we humans have been doing for hundreds of thousands of years. We design our initiation for our time and our place.

PART 8

OTHER FEATURES

People are sick and tired of being pitted against each other
when there's already so much suffering
and the Earth itself is under assault.
They're ready to reconnect and honor the life we share.
That is the great adventure of our time.

Joanna Macy

Chapter 49   Optimal Community Size

We simply do no know what size community is likely to be optimal for any grouping of people. However because we choose fewer friends vs. many acquaintances we do want to consider what might be the maximum size in which we might still contain intimacy. Tribes generally have between 30 and 150 members.

True intimacy suggests that not only must we remember the individuals who make up our group, we must also remember the relationships between them–and while the number of individuals increases arithmetically, the number of relationships grows exponentially. If we have 99 people, and add 1 more, we've only added one individual, but 99 new relationships.

The potent detail of 150 people as maximum number in community was popularized in the book **The Tipping Point**. The author Malcolm Gladwell introduces Robin Dunbar, a British anthropologist, who after studying 21 hunter-gatherer societies found that the average number of people in the village was 148.4. So the 150 **"Dunbar's Number"** is a theoretical cognitive limit to the number of people with whom one can maintain stable social relationships. These are relationships in which an individual knows who each person is, and how each person relates to every other person. Proponents assert that numbers larger than this generally require more rules, laws, and enforced norms to maintain a stable, cohesive group.

Technical explanation: If a group consists of 5 people (self + 4 others), there are 10 relationships to track: self-to-4 and 6 two-ways between pairs of others. If a group consists of 20 people (self + 19), there are 190 two-way relationships to track: self-to-19 and 171 two-ways between others. On this chart of brain densities, the human brain is theoretically capable of tracking the complexity of 147.8 relationships. Thus 150 is the approximate number of genuinely social relationships – knowing who everyone is and how they relate to me.

History: Military planners have determined that the largest functioning "fighting unit" is less than 200 men. The Hutterites, an Amish-style kinship, have a maximum of 150 people in their communities, because "otherwise people become strangers." They split off a community when the number exceeds 150.

Business application: Gore Associates, the manufacture of GoreTex and heart valves, etc., has a maximum of 150 people per manufacturing plant. As soon as they went over 150, people started to not know each other's names or jobs. They now build plants that can't fit more than 150 people, and they build another plant when capacity is reached.

Getting back to Robin Dunbar, he argued that 150 would be the mean group size for communities with a very high incentive to remain together. For a group of this size to remain cohesive, Dunbar speculated that as much as 42% of the group's time would have to be devoted to social grooming. Correspondingly, only groups under intense survival pressure, such as subsistence villages, nomadic tribes, and historical military groupings, have, on average, achieved the 150-member mark. Moreover, Dunbar noted that such groups are almost always physically close:
"... we might expect the upper limit on group size to depend on the degree of social dispersal. In dispersed societies, individuals will meet less often and will thus be less familiar with each, so group sizes should be smaller in consequence." Thus, the 150-member group would occur only because of absolute necessity — i.e., due to intense environmental and economic pressures.

This suggests that only profound economic or environmental changes might drive a community to reach 150 members. Perhaps if a community actually got near the size of 150 it might need to split into two or more smaller groups with the intent of growing deeper intimacy. Or a growing community might simply decide to stay at 32, 67 or 105 members to build and deepen the intimacy.

Each core community group might be formally connected together with other core communities, each of different sizes, visions and missions. Some will have younger or older people. They could gather and interact in creative ways with these other local core communities, such as a bi-annual surrogate grandparents and kids day, or an intercommunity picnic. These would extend our creative social system options as there are more connected people who have a trust base to share new social, economic or medical systems.

Chapter 50   Leisure Together: Playing & Praying

To have more community, we need more leisure, to make the changes to have more leisure, we need the energy of joie de vivre. But we won't have the joie without community. It's a circular association. In fact, the circle is a very nice symbol of what we're talking about because it counterpoints our usual symbol of life in corporate consumer society – the ladder.

Cecile Andrews

Leisure: If we set up our lives to get the warm inclusive community feelings we want, we might also feel like our life has slowed down. In her wonderful book *Slow Is Beautiful* (I bought a case of them) Cecile Andrews makes this connection with leisure:

> "… I'll talk about community, the core of happiness. Community is a face-to-face sharing of just and egalitarian connections with others. It's a state in which we feel accepted for our true selves and connected to others. All of these are linked, of course."

Playing with each other sounds obvious and yet as suggested in the "Alone in a Crowd" essay in chapter 24, the authentic expression of play has been wiped out, replaced by consuming stuff together. Imagine playing together as a couple dozen adults and kids all ages, getting down on all fours and without words nudging, rolling and laughing as we all literally play like puppies. We actually do this in our community and Zoe and I do it as a couple to lighten up when we get stuck. We all still have the capacity to play and we can exercise it.

Another great game we play together in our community is called "What are you doing?" All ages circle up and it starts with one person doing something and whoever is on the left says "What are you doing?" To which that one responds, describing something completely different. Example - she may have been brushing her teeth and responds to the question with "I'm climbing a tree." The asker then acts out climbing a tree for a short while when whoever in on his left says "What are you doing?" and the tree climbers says something different like "I'm wrestling alligators." The asker then proceeds to wrestle alligators until asked "What are you doing?" And so on around the circle a few times.

Elders Play: Every year my local "elders" group gathers to attend the annual Northwest MKP Elder gathering at a brothers llama ranch in Sisters, Oregon. We joke that the brothers are going to Sisters to play. And each region handles a given task; or the Puget Sound group does the food, the Corvallis bunch does the organizing and paperwork, etc. and Ashland (because we're really good at it) does the Saturday Night Live skits. We begin preparation 6 months ahead with a theme, we meet for lunch and laugh and laugh together as we imagine what gift we will surprise our brothers with this year (power, relationships, world situation). One year our theme was money and with great fun and some clever guidance we actually got 50 men to line up according to net worth. It was a very high risk exercise, yet we made it safe enough for them to circle up from debt to millionaire, each more embarrassed than the other. In the fun we also invite emotional transparency which is intrinsically healing for men. One year using a motorcycle biker theme we were able to invite our brothers to explore the depth of relationship with wives that we like to think offered insight and increased intimacy. And in all of it we laugh till we cry.

Praying: If we look historically at the qualities of successful community we often find fundamentalist religious groups which have what appears to be well bonded and happy members. However, we know these religious communities require a high level of "buy-in" to specific beliefs or creation stories. And as Neale Donald Walsh points out in his book *"What God Wants,"* many of us grew up in a religion with a "father god" who told us what "He" wanted and what we were to do.

In the last half century many millions of us observing the damage of the patriarchy have abandoned the external male authority gods and began our lifelong search for God, which has been almost vocational. And we have done well - many of us are what I might call "spiritually mature." And because we do not necessarily share religious reality constructs with each other, a new challenge has emerged.

> "Every global opinion poll shows religion declining among the youngest generation. While traditional religious affiliation is declining in the most technologically advanced societies spirituality is increasing. Spirituality refers to the very individual quest to find meaning in the broader cosmic scheme of things. ... 40% of U.S. adults describe themselves as spiritual but not religious."
>
> (Jeremy Rifkin, The Empathetic Civilization P.461)

We wonder, how do we bond with others without specific religious alignment? Many of us indeed do share a larger reality, which we identify as "spiritual," which usually means a universal perspective. The broadest of these is the "evolutionary" perspective as brilliantly presented in Michael Dowd's book *Thank God for Evolution*. Those people who find a connection easily under this vast umbrella share prayers, chants, meditations, dance and songs from all religious traditions. Because each offers a fractal element of complex sacred reality, it feels fresh and evolving.

If we stay open to all faiths, we make our selves available to many rich delights of the "soul work" from centuries of spiritual traditions. During my Warrior-Monk days in the 1990s I enjoyed the opportunity to travel for five years with an amazing Sufi character named Amir Latif. With his guidance I learned to so enjoy singing the Catholic Kýrie eléison and shabot shalom of Judaism traditions, as well as the Zikr and dances of Sufi Islamic traditions. They are all connection points to the sacred open heart and feel wonderful.

The spirituality of the evolving gift culture seems to be "open source," drawing on the past and making it up as we go. The divine unfolds every day in every way.

Together in an evolving core community we will share and co-create the joy that truly honors the Divine as we feel it within. There are hundreds of ways to kneel and kiss the ground.

Today, like every other day, we wake up empty
and frightened. Don't open the door to the study
and begin reading. Take down a musical instrument.

Let the beauty we love be what we do.
There are hundreds of ways to kneel and kiss the ground.

Jelaluddin Rumi

Chapter 51   A Personal Context & MKP History

How and why this book came to be written.

To bring a more personal perspective to this vision of "gift" community, allow me to share the MKP journey thru my eyes. This reflects the many complex steps in developing this book. I trust the stories, history and background will help integrate the vision.

Community: What I have longed for all my life. I actually had a taste of it as a kid in our little middle class town in Wisconsin. In college I wanted social connection far more that academics. I tried three fraternities, parties and even political activism. In my search I read *"Growing Up Absurd"* by Paul Goodman. As the title suggests, it validated the "disconnect" I was feeling. We were being pampered to death and asked to sell our souls. I was searching.

My Group: In the 70s my grad-school field placement and later job with a free-thinking social service agency opened the door. It was there, in my own beloved men's support group that for the first time I found authentic community beyond what I had imagined possible. I had found my passion, my mission, my "gift" and began organizing and training support groups like mini-communities.

Social Inventor: I started a business in 1977 called Small World Groups which organized people into groups which allowed them to increase their social connections. They did this both through inner growth and better social skills which made them more receptive to each other and community. Being a bit ahead of my time my "gift" was not yet strong enough to survive financially, but I began to identify my profession or life-work as "social inventor."

The "Call": As a psychotherapist in the 80s, I made a living counseling individual and couples while continuing to organize training groups. The women's movement in those days embodied the best transformational energy of that time, so I identified as a feminist therapist. Early in 1984 something quietly dramatic happened to me at a feminist therapists conference on "Interdependence." I saw so many conscious, aware women working to liberate each other that I felt somehow thunderstruck with the idea that there was nothing for men. From that moment on, my life calling became "doing something for men."

Men's Work: My epiphany led to the men's rite-of-passage training that we called the New Warrior Training Adventure (NWTA). With the poet Robert Bly as our intellectual mentor, Ron Hering, Rich Tosi and I focused our attention and opened our hearts enough to allow this initiatory work to flow through us into the world. We had each done a lot of inner work and the results showed as we were able to hold space for other men to open to big learning very quickly.

Integrations Groups: Seeing the potency of the training, we realized that the men needed time and safe space together to "integrate" the learning. I had been creating similar groups for years, so our on-going support groups were soon developed. These affectionately named "I-groups" allow men to continue refining their new skills. Many of these groups have gone on for many years even decades. These bonded groups often form a base for local community.

A Circle of Men: The Book: Seeing the need beyond the NWTA for information on how to build men's groups I finished and published my book called *A Circle of Men: The Original Manuel for Men's Support Groups.* In my book's introduction I talk about my passion for community and my history. That was 1992 and I'm still struggling to make something tangible of this undying vision of community

Sudden Growth: By the early 90s we had developed training centers coast to coast, just about the time Robert Bly's book *Iron John* sold a million copies. Men were hungry for something and the number of our centers tripled quickly. It was obvious that we held something men really wanted. To feel our own deep sense of manhood blessed by other men is archetypal. Finding our hearts, trusting other men and feeling our life mission come alive, all serve to bring men to a significant new way of being.

Serendipity: A specious incident very early in our history yielded unexpected gifts. Two men attempted to "steal" the work from the founders. A clever ruse couched in brotherly trust turned the control of our work over to another legal entity. Feeling the deceit, Rich Tosi as president literally gave away the NWTA by adding seven new centers, and instantly it was owned by all. Thus, this first gift set a huge precedent by the founders of the "give-away" which became a heart felt ethic in our brotherhood. We often say that we "live the give-away." which is reflected perfectly in our transpersonal missions of service.

Vampires: The second gift came from my deep wondering about just how could these men who called us "brothers" do something so obviously criminal. Much

143

research led to the discovery that the vampire (known by many names, most of them psychiatric like psychopath) is a human type that has existed throughout history. My study came together as a talk at the 2000 Hartland Men's Conference called "Mean People Suck: How Psychic Vampires Touch Your Life." The tape was sent out to hundreds of our leaders which led to an awareness that as men step up to leadership we need to truly check each other out. We call it "hot-seating" and I'm proud to say it has kept us as a large international organization very atypically clean in our leadership.

NWTA protocols: In the middle 90s our initiatory work was expanding such that the form in which the training was delivered needed to be formally codified. I took on the formidable task of writing it all out in detail, and in 1994 I rewrote the whole thing again with specific "intentions" so the staff-men on trainings knew not only what to do but precisely why. It was ritually gifted to the MKP Leader Body for safe-keeping.

Identity Expansion: By the late 90s we had outgrown our name New Warrior Network. We put out a call around the world for a new name. A brother from Louisville Kentucky was on his morning jog when the name "ManKind Project" with the capital "K" showed up. At the next annual meeting we sifted and sorted thru hundreds of names. Suddenly the lights inexplicably went out and when we emerged from the darkness, there was a decision. It was obvious to all of us that we had our new name.

The ManKind Project: Our new name reflects the capacity of men to work with kindness. From the very beginning as founders we worked as peers trusting our best gifts to be recognized and tested. And though over the years we have established some hierarchal structure to guide an international organization, we have continued to work largely by consensus. This means we trust the wisdom of the group. I have watched each year as we learned little by little how to lead with our hearts and take care not to get polarized. Each year we have gained more and more skills learning how to lead with love.

Leaders, Elders and Lodge Keepers: As groups of men bonded according to their passions, unique structures kept showing up. The training leaders began to gather to insure high quality leadership and leader training and became the Leader Body. The elder men knew they could bring the wisdom of experience into our work in a healthy way and the Elder Council formed. At the same time our unique shamans from around the world gathered to bring in the indigenous wisdom of the ages in a good way and they came to be know as Lodge Keepers. Some years ago

144

there was some heated discussion as to which of these groups held the true "spiritual" energy for MKP. After some intense sharing and listening they decided on a "braid" as symbolic as the three woven strands much stronger than any alone.

Powerful Sisters: Early on in our men's work our women friends and partners began asking for a training experience for them. Char Tosi courageously began step-by-step building the Woman Within training and taking it to communities around the world. It is a heart opening "lover" training in which women learn to heal, bond with and deeply trust other women. Some years later Sarah Schley who had been in the military, gathered some Shadow Work trained women to co-create Women in Power, a full-out "warrior" initiatory training for women.

The part of me that feels the painful weight of the patriarchy silencing women for far too long feels joyful that these sisters have been inspired to create their own excellent work.

Visionary: After a decade or so the MKP brotherhood asked me what gift I wanted as a founder. I said I wanted a seat on the council, a modest stipend and the title Visionary-at-Large because it sounded so cool. I took my new title quite seriously and studied intensely the "state of the world." Also I paid attention to how we might talk about what we as MKP actually do. The following is some of how I have come to understand the breadth and beauty of what we actually do, especially in regard to building social capital.

Bowling Alone: The phrase "social capital" showed up for me in the book *Bowling Alone*, written by Robert Putnam a professor of Public Policy at Harvard University, and published in 2000. He has shown most dramatically the value of social capital as the trust that binds people together. It's the understood mutual support, cooperation and reciprocity in relationships. Think of it as "face to face" with shared vibrational resonance. It's literally the glue of society.

A Time of Need: Robert Putnam shows that 120 years ago social capital in US culture was seriously reduced by urbanization, industrialization and immigration. Faced with this challenge the county righted itself. Within a few decades, a range of "social inventions" were created, from the Red Cross, Boy Scouts, YMCA and Urban League to many of the great fraternal organizations: the Moose, Elks, Lions, Optimists, Odd Fellows, Rotary, Kiwanis, the Knights of Pythias and the VFW. All contributed to rebuilding social capital. Putnam goes on to graphically show how as the century wore on, the majority of these groups, except for a brief post WWII resurgence, have declined or become virtually obsolete.

3,000,000 hours of Social Capital: As a math experiment, imagine 25 initiates plus 38 men staffing 120 NWTA 40 hours weekends equals over 300,000 hours of annual social capital. Then consider that 1000 integration groups with ten men for 3 hours, meeting 50 weeks per year equals one and a half million hours of social capital time. When we add in leader trainings, open house intros, welcome home graduations, all the spin off training events (Woman Within, Women In Power, Boys to Men. Etc.) it quickly adds up to well over 3 million hours of solid social capital each year infused into our culture. And as people now comfortable with intimate social contact take their skills into the world, they inadvertently produce more social capital every day, which probably generates another million hours each year. All stemming from one small circle of men!

Social Impact of Belonging: So, what might we actually be doing in the world by building social capital? Putnam's work shows how social bonds are the most powerful predictors of life satisfaction. For example, he reports that getting married is equivalent to quadrupling your income and attending a club meeting regularly is equivalent to doubling your income. When there is a loss of social capital it is felt in critical ways: Communities with less social capital have lower educational performance and more teen pregnancy, child suicide, low birth weight, and prenatal mortality. Social capital is also a strong predictor of crime rates and other measures of neighborhood quality of life, as it is of our physical health. In quantitative terms, if you both smoke and belong to no groups, it's a close call as to which is the riskier behavior."

MKP as social invention: In so many ways MKP may be seen as an archetypal example of a social invention generating social capital. It started from a felt need in society. It grew organically and in a non-hierarchal way from the men who experienced the power and transformation in their own lives. It is strongly volunteer based - men are eager to give back the gift they have received. It is common to have many more men than needed applying to volunteer and pay their own way to serve as staff for the next group of men taking the training in their area. Many men also have paid their own way to go to South Africa or New Zealand to help staff the trainings and launch those centers. It is a profound labor of love and service.

MKP at 25: A quarter century later The ManKind Project has established 40 strong active communities in 8 countries around the world and has served well nearly 50,000 men. Ten thousand men sit in weekly support groups, growing, learning and nurturing our "missions of service" as we generate hundreds of new projects each year.

MKP building community: If we define community as any grouping of people who know and trust each other it's easy to see the thousands of "communities" that are now in the world as a result of MKP. Because most of the men of MKP have been tested in the fires of the NWTA and it's follow up I-Groups for some years they have an atypically high level of trust. They have embodied a fairly sophisticated skill-set which includes intimate communications, emotional literacy and conflict resolution. This is what allows the exceptional level of trust and safety that develops in a relatively short time period of months or years as opposed to decades. How can we measure the success of this work?

Serving the Soul: MKP is obviously doing something which "speaks" to people of the new culture during a time of increased alienation. I believe people are literally dying for social connections. Everything in our culture mitigates against personal face to face contact. We actually need this contact for survival. We need to feel the resonant field of other human beings a minimum of once every 7 days or we start to forget who we are. Interesting that churches of all types meet every week. It is what keeps us humans...well human.

Visionary Report: Each year at the annual meeting I get to report to my brothers what I see from my research and observations. Year after year as I dug deeper down the rabbit hole of the state of the world, I would return saying " Brothers, remember how bad I said it was back last year, well it's worse." There was very little receptive listening for what I had to say in the early days. It got so bad that I even took the totem name "Delusional Duck" as a way of stepping into the projected shadow, doing whatever it might take as long as it increased the chance that they might hear the message.

Lifeboats Tour: Having studied intensely as the "visionary," I could see the environmental, energy and economic collapse as inevitable. I took my "early warning" Lifeboat Tour on the road in 2005, visiting 25 cities, where we met in groups of 15 to 50 men and women. Everywhere I went I could feel the fear and the longing for community. I became devoted to learning how to provide the community that they seemed to be longing for. I opened a project and website called Sacred Lifeboats. However, the concept of a "Lifeboat Community" felt too survival focused, raising questions of competing for food and other resources. Something else was needed.

Attempts at Community. The list of my community experiments that did not work is long and frustrating. When I talk about my having "failed" my friends tell me to stop using the word "fail." I do know that Thomas Edison failed ten thousand times before he got the light bulb right. And I fully understand the deep learning that comes from the willingness to take the risk and "fail." I love the phrase "failing forward" and do get that with each new experiment I'm learning something even if it is "what doesn't work."

Relentless Optimists: One of the thousand MKP groups currently meeting each week somewhere around the world is my own team of five men. We call ourselves the Relentless Optimists, and the joke is that as worldly, savvy guys we know it is far to late and things are far too bad for pessimism. Thus our name and our chosen task is to support each other in building social inventions. Over the decade that we have been together we have written a stack of books, generated the annual holiday "Abundance Swap," Heart Circles, seminars, great service projects and an awesome number of gatherings. We get stuff done because we have the fierce love and support which makes it so much more fun.

Adoring the Goddess: When I began my inner work back in the 1970s I recognized that this "growth" process would go on as long as I was willing to stay open and keep learning. Now in my 60s, I was able to open my heart enough to receive the feminine. A week long, very intense training called *Clearing the Air* run by Gordon Clay and Shauna Wilson gave me a huge experience of safe intimacy between men and women. Zoe, who had already done this work, showed up ready to stand with me and receive my love. I found my Goddess in physical form. Finally mature enough to choose and commit to a woman has been the joy of my life. I'm finding that our love is not atypical as I often meet men now who just flat out adore their wives. This suggests that the time has come for intimate communities of men and women. Thus this book.

My Sisters and Brothers are ready: I see the readiness of my sisters who have done their deep inner work. They are ready to put down the sword as they claim their power. I feel the readiness in the men of MKP to move into this next social maturity step. As "initiators of men" we do very well. The descent is deep, the ordeal fierce and the return into men's community becomes precious to most brothers. Now, the challenge of true long-term community with both men and women stands waiting. We have the skills, vision and volition.

Home Town Community: Many of us here in Ashland, Oregon have lots of friends and a good healthy sense of local community. There are several hundred "warrior brothers" (MKP men) who live here. We enjoy the flow in and out of various sub-communities. It feels free and easy as our paths cross every month or so. We care for each other in a good way and have a very high sense of belonging to something like community. I envision much more.

Gift Community: Because the men of MKP have cultivated an inner sense of the "living the give–away" I believe we have the essential qualities of consciousness which this book is calling forth. Many of us have Gift Community in our hearts as we live our daily lives bringing our gifts to others and expecting the natural reciprocation.

World is waiting: Imagine, women and men ready and wanting to give our gift. The world is waiting and we know the joyous experience of grace when we expand just a bit. Gift communities of men and women, embracing the worthy task of co-creating the new world, are calling to us. We are the people. Now is the time.

Chapter 52   Gratitude: Living Into Our Gifts

Most people expect to get happy and then become grateful for this happiness. This makes perfect, logical sense, but it's completely backwards. That's not how the spiritual path works. The empowerment of your life is to become grateful first, and then happiness follows.   Brother David Steindl-Rast

"Gratitude is a revolutionary act!"   I don't know where this wise gift of an observation came from, but it's profound as we participate in this adventure of the evolving gift culture. It is the perfect response to the axiom: **"We can never get enough of what we don't really need."**

The old story sells us an infinite amount of that which can never truly fill us. The only thing that cannot be bought and sold is love or volitional attention. And only in a container of love do we find relationships of joy. Our new story of the gift community is all about co-creating truly safe containers for the dynamic unfolding process of authentic intimate relationships. The emotion of gratitude flows from these relationships. Living in gratitude changes everything as our hearts open and open and open.

If we build it with care our gift community will hold us gently and fiercely as we heal and open our hearts, more often, more deeply.
This is how we get what we truly want; love, family, friends and true community. Most everything else is salve to cover the wounds.

Women and men coming together to consciously co-create something fresh and new. Communities of people who really need each other, giving their gifts, generating the needed social and other inventions.

This is rare in the social complexity of our time. Ask what do you really want. What is your gift? It starts now. Reach out, make that first call.

AFTERWORD

RESOURCES

Love has nothing to do with what
you are expecting to get --
only with what you are expecting to give --
- which is everything.

--Katherine Hepburn

Book List of Recommendations:

These books have most influenced my work, research and creative process. Because I cherish "the truth" as best I can perceive it, I have taken the time and energy to get to know and trust several of these authors. I have ordered the list according to publications date, newest first. Enjoy!

Sacred Economics: Money, Gift, and Society in the Age of Transition, Charles Eisenstein, 2011, North Atlantic Books, $22.95

Navigating The Coming Chaos: A Handbook For Inner Transition, Carolyn Baker, 2011, iUniverse, Inc., $25.95

The Abundant Community: Awakening the Power of Families and Neighborhoods, John McKnight & Peter Block, 2010, Berrett-Koehler Publishers, $26.95

What's Mine Is Yours: The Rise of Collaborative Consumption, Rachel Botsman & Roo Rogers, 2010, HarperCollins Publishers, $26.99

The Story of Stuff: How Our Obsession with Stuff Is Trashing the Planet, Our Communities, and Our Health-and a Vision for Change, Annie Leonard, 2010, Free Press, $26.00   http://www.storyofstuff.org/

Hope and Hard Times: Communities, Collaboration and Sustainability, Ted Bernard, 2010, New Society Publishers, $19.95

The Transition Handbook: From Oil Dependence to Local Resilience, Rob Hopkins, 2009, Chelsea Green Publishing, $24.95

The Empathetic Civilizations: The Race to Global Consciousness in A World in Crisis, Jeremy Rifkin, 2009, Jeremy P. Tarcher/Penguin, $27.95

Plan B 4.0: Mobilizing to Save Civilization, Lester Brown, 2009, Norton, $29.95

The Living Universe: Where are we? Who are we? Where are we going? Duane Elgin, 2009, Berrett-Koehler Publishers, $15.95

Sacred Demise: Walking the Spiritual Path of Industrial Civilization's Collapse, Carolyn Baker, 2009, iUniverse, $25.95

Agenda for a New Economy: From Phantom Wealth to Real Wealth, David Korten, 2009, Berrett-Koehler Publishers, $14.95

Social Change 2.0: A Blueprint for Reinventing Our World, David Gershon, 2009, High Point/Chelsea Green, $27.95

The Hope: A Guide to Sacred Activism, Andrew Harvey, 2009, Hay House, $16.95

Empire of Illusion: The End of Literacy and the Triumph of Spectacle, Chris Hedges, 2009, Nation Books, $24.95

The Ascent of Humanity: The Age of Separation, the Age of Reunion, and the Convergence of Crises that is birthing the transition, Charles Eisenstein, 2008, Panenthea Press, $25.00

Community: The Structure of Belonging, Peter Block, 2008, Berrett-Koehler Publishers, $26.95

Plan "C": Community Survival Strategies for Peak Oil and Climate Change, Pat Murphy, 2008, New Society Publishers, $19.95

The Long Descent: A Users Guide to the End of the Industrial Age, John Michael Greer, 2008, New Society Publishers, $18.95

Culturequake: The End of Modern Culture and the Birth of a New World, Chuck Burr, 2008, Trafford Publishing, $19.95

Peak Everything: Waking Up to the Century of Declines, Richard Heinberg, 2007, New Society Publishers, $24.95

Blessed Unrest: How the Largest Movement in the World Came into Being and Why No One Saw It Coming, Paul Hawken, 2007, Viking, $24.95

Thank God for Evolution: How the Marriage of Science and Religion Will Transform Your Life and Our World, Michael Dowd, 2007, Viking, $24.95

Creating Community Anywhere: Finding Support and Connection in a Fragmented World, Carolyn Shaffer & Kristen Anundsen,1993-2005, CCC Press, $20.00

Finding Community: How to Join an Ecovillage or Intentional Community, Diana Leafe Christian, New Society Publishers, 2007, $24.95

Slow is Beautiful: New Visions of Community, Leisure and Joie de Vivre Cecile Andrews, 2006, New Society Publishers, $16.95

The Great Turning: from Empire to Earth Community, By: David Korten, 2006, Berrett-Koehler Publishers & Kumarian Press, $27.95 Hardback

Ecovillage Ithaca, Liz Walker, New Society Publishers, 2005, $17.95

Speak Peace in a World of Conflict, Marshall B Rosenberg PhD, 2005, PuddleDancer Press, $17.95

Waking the Global Heart: Humanity's Rite of Passage from the Love of Power to the Power of Love, Anodea Judith, 2006, Elite Books, Santa Rosa, $17.95

The Translucent Revolution: How People Just Like You Are Waking Up and Changing the World, Arjuna Ardagh, 2005. New World Library, $16.95

Powerdown: Options and Actions for a Post-carbon World, Richard Heinberg, 2004, New Society Publishers, $16.95,

Creating a Life Together: Practical Tools to Grow Ecovillages and Intentional Communities, Diana Leafe Christian, New Society Publishers, 2003, $22.95

Beyond Civilization: Humanity's Next Great Adventure, Daniel Quinn, Harmony Books: New York, 1999, $21.95

Unholy Hungers: Encountering the Psychic Vampire in Ourselves and Others, Barbara Hort, Shambala Press, 1996, $16.00

The Gift: Imagination and the Erotic Life of Property, Lewis Hyde, Vintage Books, 1983, $15.00

Websites:

We believe that we actually need to know the state of our world as a base from which to learn and take action. Therefore we suggest these sites and presentations as some of the very best we've discovered.

SOCIAL ARTISTS, ARCHITECTS & ENTREPRENEURS:

Jean Houston created the Social Artistry Leadership Institute seminar 10 years ago to enhance human capacities in the light of social complexity.
http://www.jeanhouston.org/socialartistry-whatitis-new.cfm

Jim Channon supports social architectures who focus on culturally significant purposeful creation. His work with the military (see film: Men Who Stare at Goats) inspired the author with the words "Warrior Monk" in the mid-90s.
http://arcturus.org/arcturus3/?q=node/2

David Gershon has a stunning track record of generating what he calls social entrepreneurship as seen brilliantly in his newest book *Social Change 2.0: A Blueprint for Reinventing Our World,*
http://www.socialchange2.com/index.php/home

TRAININGS FOR MEN & WOMEN:

The ManKind Project: Now in our 26th year – Enjoy. http://mankindproject.org/

Woman Within: Excellent archetypal "Lover" training for women.
http://www.womanwithin.org/

Women in Power: Excellent archetypal "Warrior" training for women.
 http://www.womeninpowerprogram.com/

Alison Armstrong is extraordinarily brilliant in helping women truly see men in her work called Celebrating Men, Satisfying Women®
http://www.understandmen.com/index.html

A Culture of Honoring: The best reclaiming of both healthy masculine and feminine energies we have found. http://www.cultureofhonouring.com/

TAKING ACTION:

http://www.transitionnetwork.org/ **The Transition Towns** movement feels like one of the best things going right now. Only 5 years old, it has swept the planet. I've met a co-founder and key author (MKP Brothers) who feels solid, visionary & committed.

NEWS:

http://www.commondreams.org/ Excellent progressive news source.

http://carolynbaker.net   In this digest **Carolyn Baker** speaks her truth to power with a day by day synopsis of the on-going contraction of all systems, often introducing brilliant writers and researchers.

http://www.globalresearch.ca/index.php?context=home "In an era of media disinformation, our focus has essentially been to center on the 'unspoken truth'." **The Centre for Research on Globalization** is an independent registered non profit organization and media group of writers, scholars and journalists based in Montreal, Quebec, Canada.

http://thearchdruidreport.blogspot.com/ The very thoughtful blog is written by **John Michael Greer,** a friend, prolific author and druid. I much respect his clear, earthy yet almost transcendent insights.

ECONOMY: http://www.chrismartenson.com/ **Chris Martinson** is a PhD, former Fortune 300 VP who states "The next 20 years will be unlike anything we have ever seen." He gets 10,000 hits per day on his web site. Please take the time to study this exquisitely well done *Crash Course*, which is free. Chris focuses on Economy, Energy & Environment as he suggests enough urgency that you will understand: "I NEED my neighbors!"

Reciprocity: Part of the Gift

In Lewis Hyde's classic book, called *The Gift*, he speaks of "reciprocity" as returning a gift, going to and fro between people (the root words are re and pro, back and forth). Reciprocal giving is the simple form of gift exchange. When the gift moves into a circle, with at least three points, no one ever receives it from the same person who gave it. *"When I give to someone from whom I do not receive (and yet I receive elsewhere), it's as if the gift goes around a corner before it comes back. I have to give blindly. And I will feel a sort of blind gratitude as well."*

For 15 years I have been living the gift. I have offered training retreats in several countries around the world and always delivered my service first, then asked for a gift contribution at the end. Like most of us receiving was harder than giving, so I consciously used my Warrior Monk training to take on the challenge of receiving love and money. For years, I practicing receiving love at the end of every Warrior Monk day and receiving money at the end of each training. I always cried. To truly receive breaks the heart open.

I trust the value of my work as a contribution to people's lives. I invite people to consider their ability to pay, the value received and interest in supporting my work in the world. This book is my gift, it's what I do. It is a social invention offered to you by a life long social entrepreneur. It has been in the works for several years ad my passion, joy and burden in full recognition of the need for it in the world.

It is too valuable to hold back in any way. I give it to you to have and to use.

And if it feels right for you to support us and our work, please send a contribution – gift in any amount that feels right to you. Some options:
1. Use my Paypal account on our website: giftcommunity.net
2. Send a check: Bill Kauth, 258 Greenbriar Pl., Ashland, OR 97520
3. Accept this book as a gift and Pay It Forward as you can.

Finally: our sentiments reflected in the words of our friend Charles Eisenstien:
> *"A time is coming when we will shift from a profit-taking economy to a gift economy, from an economy of 'how can I take the most?' to 'how can I best give of my gifts?"*

Biographies

Bill Kauth and Zoe Alowan

Bill and Zoe have been working together, actively learning and teaching the concepts and processes of Gift Community. They are committed to bringing about a healing understanding of the essential feminine and masculine with a focus on building communities of men and women.

Zoe

Zoe Alowan has been actively engaged in sacred art for many decades. As a painter, sculptor, dancer and story teller, her work explores transformation and healing. Her life is about reclaiming essence wisdom She utilizes the inspiration of the divine feminine, humor, song and ritual movement as ways of celebrating wholeness. She has taught at Esalen and Naropa Institute, facilitates women's groups, singing circles as well as intuitive process painting retreats.

Bill

Bill Kauth was working as a psychotherapist and business consultant in 1984 when he conceived and co-founded the New Warrior Training Adventure, now presented by The ManKind Project to nearly 50,000 men in 40 centers in 8 countries around the world. In 1992 St. Martin's Press published his book *A Circle of Men: The Original Manual for Men's Support Groups.* As a social inventor over the last two decades, Bill also co-founded the Spiritual Warrior, Inner King Training and in 1995 launched the Warrior-Monk Training Retreat.

Made in the USA
San Bernardino, CA
08 February 2020